BROKEN NO MORE

A true story of abuse, amnesia, and finding God's love

BROKEN NO MORE

A true story of abuse, amnesia, and finding God's love

S. DAWN BRADFORD

This is a work of creative nonfiction. The events herein are portrayed to the best of the author's memory. While all the stories in this book are true, some names and identifying details may have been changed to protect the privacy of the people involved.

Editorial work and production management by Eschler Editing
Cover design by Jennifer Elliot
Interior print design and layout by Sydnee Hyer
eBook design and layout by Sydnee Hyer
Production services facilitated by Scrivener Books

Published by Rise Up

ISBN: 978-1-949165-19-7

To Chad and Linda, who provided unfailing support every step of my journey

CONTENT WARNING

This book includes references to or scenes that contain sexual violence (including rape, sexual abuse/assault, pedophilia), cult/ritualistic abuse, torture, toxic relationships, anxiety, memory repression, depression, guilt, and manipulation.

CONTENTS

FOREWORD

They say the body remembers that which the mind forgets, or more accurately, what the mind protects us from. A violation of trust, a violation of our childlike expectations that the world is safe, a violation of that intrinsic contract we all executed when we squalled into physical form and took that breath of life. Violation–that is the source of all personal mire. And it is when a fundamental violation of our humanity occurs that a psyche can shatter. But the body remembers.

I've never known a person who has endured more or paid a higher price than S. Dawn Bradford. And she has come out the other side a rebirthed human being. Dawn faced her own dark night of the soul and bravely fought her own watery grave so that she might heal–and so that she might also share her discoveries and that new light with others.

When a fundamental violation is mended, there may be years of damage to restore, but the hunger for justice can shift. We find that the mighty eternal scales finally balance when our personal Gethsemanes give us access to healing, not only for ourselves but for our brothers and sisters who live in this inequitable world with us.

In *Broken No More,* Dawn shares her unspeakable trials, and she also forges a path for all of us. What is broken, even a psyche, can be healed. When we heal, we come back with a gift that only those of us who've experienced deep traumatic wounds and have excavated our souls can know. And as it is with all gifts, they are meant to be given away. When we give, we empty the vessel to receive. When we finally experience this principle, what we find is a wellspring of new life. While the trauma may have been secreted away in our minds, the answers have been whispering from within all along. The body remembers, and the soul forgives.

—ANGIE FENIMORE, INTERNATIONALLY
BEST-SELLING AUTHOR

PREFACE

I am afraid of whales. And everything else in the ocean, but especially whales. Even an accidental flick of a giant tail could kill me. Compared to the ocean I'm a gnat. I can see myself treading water, alone, in the expanse. Danger lurks only feet away, but I can't see it. I refuse to give up and sink below the glassy surface because I'm afraid of drowning and the creatures in the water. Rescue helicopters never find the little gnat and I drown anyway. To me, Hell is not on fire, it is under water.

Most of my life has been lived in fear. Fear of rotting in a foreign prison while travelling, being humiliated in a restaurant, and suffering a thousand varieties of horrific deaths. Everyone has fears. It's normal. Only, I found out my fears weren't normal. Regular people aren't terrified of being in the wrong place at the wrong time and being convicted of a crime they didn't commit. They don't spend hundreds of hours imagining every conceivable way they might die and praying that when it happens, God grants a less terrifying death.

Normal people don't have dreams of being attacked by an electric octopus intent on killing them, who can only be temporarily stunned by rubber bands, but is otherwise indestructible. My nights were filled with animals, like when I hid in a house while a fifteen foot tall mama buffalo battered it to get to me because she thought I killed her baby.

No matter how safe a dream started, it always transformed into a nightmare showcasing my helplessness against something larger or smarter. My dreams were a mirror of my days, only more interesting. I moved through life in varying degrees of depression and anxiety, trying to prevent strangers, friends, and family from hurting me and often failing at the attempt. As I got older, the support of my second husband, medication, and regular therapy helped me enter the realm of normal functioning. The more I understood, the more my life didn't make sense.

I was thirty-nine before I wondered why I married my first husband despite knowing, as I walked down the aisle, that it was the biggest mistake of my life. I told people I hadn't wanted to waste my parents' money, but the entire day cost six hundred dollars thanks to a small wedding in their living room. The real reason was that I believed at the tender age of nineteen that premarital sex was a sin and that the only way to make it right was to get married to him, even though I hadn't gotten pregnant. In my middle-aged wisdom, even that notion made little sense, especially since my family and I hardly attended church at the time.

As I continued therapy, I gained more questions than answers about my life. Unanswered questions bother me, so I began digging into my past relationships, and then into my childhood. My therapist taught me the non-dominant hand technique to help me remember. I asked a question and then using my left, non-dominant hand, my inner child wrote or drew the answer.

I enjoyed getting to know my life better until Saturday, July 30, 2016.

I locked my door and sat on my bed with paper and colored pencils to begin another session with my inner child. I picked out a black colored pencil and began to draw a happy little girl with tiny arms and legs. Then I drew a door. On the other side of the door was a tall figure with evil eyes and a big smile. On the bottom I wrote, "Come in, little girl."

A sickly sensation began in my gut and spread outward. As more images emerged, I tried to force my hand to draw something else, but my inner child had taken over and I watched in horror as twenty-three pages spilled out in pictures and words detailing that I'd been molested as a child. I even drew the scene of a grown woman who walked in and caught us. She called me a whore and a tramp, though I was too young to know what those words meant. She told me I ought to be ashamed and that good girls keep their clothes on.

I was no longer a middle-aged housewife, I was a child who understood for the first time that she was not a good girl, but a bad girl. I felt the weight of that lie as it grew over the years and how I'd fought against it. I never imagined the roots came from a woman who blamed me rather than helping me.

I dropped my pen as if it were an ember and looked up. The crisp lines of my dresser swayed in a fuzzy dance. My head felt detached from my body, in danger of floating away. I couldn't face my children or think clearly enough to function like a normal person, so I ran away for two days until the initial shock had worn off.

July 30, 2016 was the day I began spinning my cocoon. I didn't know then what happens to a caterpillar to magically turn itself into a butterfly. Inside the cocoon, the caterpillar digests itself, creating a nutritious, organized soup. Floating inside are genetically coded discs which feed off the soup and develop into each part of the adult butterfly. It's kind of like playing with Legos. A child can break down a structure and rebuild it into something new. Every caterpillar holds within it everything it needs to become a butterfly, but most will not survive long enough for this final stage. When the process is complete, the butterfly has to free itself from its self-made prison. If it doesn't get out, it dies. If someone helps it out, it will never fly. Every butterfly is a miracle of strength and endurance.

I was never satisfied as a caterpillar. I was born to fly.

1
CHILDHOOD

Mom thought she was crazy when I began to kick inside her. No matter how she tried to remind her brain she'd suffered a miscarriage, the sensations didn't go away. Her doctor confirmed I was alive, and explained she must have miscarried a fraternal twin. Four months later she gave birth to a fighter.

My childhood is a collection of broken fragments of memories. The three homes in Idaho have been reduced to the single image of a black dog knocking me down when I was three.

A small town in Colorado holds the most memories. I sat on the front step of our house crying every morning because Mom locked the door to force me to go to kindergarten. By second-grade, my class photo shows an adorable blonde surrounded by abundant friends of many cultures and religious backgrounds.

The memories of Gilcrest, Colorado flood in. The pickled face of a friend's grandmother offering me store-bought brownies in exchange for a kiss. I'd agonized until my eyes glimpsed the coveted treat enshrined in its thin plastic container. I remember those final few seconds as her bright ruby lipstick neared and I realized she meant to kiss me on the lips. I froze, but she continued, her stale breath assaulting my senses, until my smooth lips touched her leathery ones. I'd sold my soul for a frosting-coated bit of heaven.

Another friend, Russell, and I sat cross-legged, discussing death, on the hot asphalt in the middle of the road. It had been his idea, and I'd been taught to let my friends choose our activities. I made sure to look both ways before I walked into the street and sat down. It tasted deliciously dangerous, and I was hooked. Numerous times we sat there, exploring through conversation what it might feel like to get hit by a car, where our spirits went when the body died, and what we might do when we arrived there.

My bravery vanished when a large car crept around the corner and lumbered down our street of tract housing. We'd jumped up and scampered away, neither of us eager to get the answers to our questions that day. I knew then that I was a coward and we'd never been in any danger.

I remember nothing of the house I lived in on that road. I'm pretty sure I spent all my waking time at my best friend, Katie's, trailer. She was the luckiest girl I knew, with store-bought clothes, a dream house for Barbie, and a salon in the other half of their double-wide. Vibrant scenes of my time with Katie slip past: summers spent swimming in the community pool, doing each other's blonde hair in the salon after it closed, and watching my first scary movie. Katie and I spent every spare moment of a glorious eighteen months together until I finished third grade and Dad moved us to Utah. I never saw Katie again.

That first summer in Utah, my family and I camped out on my aunt's enclosed porch until Dad found a job selling tractors. Mom drove us to a tiny town in Cache Valley and pulled to a stop in front of an ancient pale-green house that emerged from a sea of knee-high wild grass. We couldn't afford the central heat, so Grandpa welded a few spare parts into a woodburning stove that looked like a giant black pig with long, spindly legs and a pipe for a tail to vent the smoke out of the house.

Mom said we were poorer than church mice, but I always figured the mice ate better than we did. My candy was the raw milk our neighbor traded for storing her hay in the barn behind the house. I constantly begged for more than the one small cup we were allowed from the metal jug each day.

I remember that hot summer day Dad sold a tractor and Mom was able to go grocery shopping. She brought home a little cardboard container of ice cream. After dinner, we all gathered around the small Formica table to get our share. Shouts of "I'm bigger, so it takes more to fill me up," and "No fair! I deserve just as much as they do!" rang out.

"I'm going to cut it equally," Mom said in a firm voice she rarely used. "It's the only way to be fair." Silence descended as she peeled away the thin cardboard covering, revealing the naked rectangle of vanilla in all its glory. She pulled out a long bread knife and carefully sliced the rectangle in half, then proceeded to divide each half into four equal pieces. With eight of us, each child kept eagle eyes out for which piece was slightly larger than the others.

I savored each spoonful of my slice despite the heat of the house melting the edges because I had no idea how long it would be before we got another treat.

I remember the ice cream, but I have no hint of when the pressure cooker blew up, burning my mother's face and knocking out one of her front teeth. I also remember the day we started receiving free school lunch. The food was so good I couldn't understand why Mom had waited so long or why she hated getting it for free.

By the end of our year there, my only pair of pants had holes in the knees, we were used to the dehydrated butter and other disgusting items found in our food storage, and the bank had foreclosed on the house.

Dad found a job at a ranch; it came with a regular paycheck and a house. We quickly dubbed it Rattlesnake Ranch but spent our time climbing the mountain in our backyard despite the snakes. Tired of being poor, Mom got a teaching scholarship and enrolled in college. I remember two things from that year: Dad yelling a lot and our scrappy mutt Benji getting killed by the neighbor's blue heeler.

Before long, Dad switched jobs again, and we moved to another isolated house near what became a bird refuge when conservationism became popular. Back then it was simply a farming community where fields outnumbered houses, and we were considered outsiders. Our tiny prefabricated house sat at the end of a dirt road. My four brothers used the bunk beds in the largest room, my sister and I shared the smallest room and a bed, and my parents got the last room. Half a mile west, where our lane met the narrow asphalt road that served the area, two houses were nestled together. My sister and I often walked down the lane to play with the kids who lived there, but she got mad at me because I always sneaked off to play with the older boys instead of with her and the girls.

We had no money, but we had brains. My two oldest brothers left home by earning good grades and full scholarships, which meant I finally got my own bed. I wasn't smart enough for that path, so I learned housekeeping skills by taking over the cooking and cleaning while Mom put in long hours as a high school teacher.

I survived middle school and made it through my freshman year of high school. I don't know why my parents let me move into our shed or why I decided it was a good idea, but I happily left my bossy older sister behind. In exchange for my freedom, I put up with a body covered in swollen spider bites.

A month into my sophomore year, Mom got a job in Salt Lake City and we moved again. I traded the mice and spiders for the sounds of cars speeding past my window day and night. Mom put in long hours moving up the corporate ladder while Dad sold office supplies. I don't know if Mom's success bothered Dad or if it was because he was the only one who still attended services at The Church of Jesus Christ of Latter-Day Saints, known as the Mormon church, but the fights that had been going on for years between my parents intensified.

Abandoned to fend for myself, I withdrew and became isolated as I tried to navigate the landscape of a foreign big-city environment. Darkness invaded my life. I went from sweet little girl to sullen teen overnight. I cut off the hair that trailed down my back, took up swearing, and skipped school. I learned to be a chameleon, adapting to the roles adults or peers expected me to fill when I was around them. I figured out what the teachers wanted and got good grades for the first time in my life. Few people noticed that, by my junior year, high school was actually shredding my soul.

My English teacher did notice and, concerned, reported it to the school counselor, who called Mom. I didn't know how to tell her something was wrong inside my brain, so I shrugged it off and pretended I was fine.

During my senior year, suicidal thoughts took over, and I began planning my death. I reviewed every possible avenue for hurting myself. Dad owned guns, and Mom kept knives in the kitchen, but I didn't want to leave a mess for Mom. I decided huge doses of mixed pills and a rarely used public bathroom were the how and where. I planned my funeral, daydreaming for hours about what each person would say. I only needed to pick the day.

As I lay there thinking about my options one day, my mind shifted to what would come when I died. I pictured myself standing in front of Jesus to see if I believed there was anything after this life.

Suddenly, it wasn't my imagination. I was looking at Jesus, and he was looking at me with a mixture of love and sadness, understanding and disappointment. I couldn't open my mouth to tell him I had murdered myself and cut short his plan for me.

My ceiling came back into focus, and pain flooded my heart. I knew the dark chaos in my mind would follow me to the other side. There was no escaping. I withered under the truth, turning my anger to God for taking away the only hope I had—the only way out of my pain. Something was wrong with me, and I didn't know why it was there or how to fix it.

I graduated, bought my first car, and began attending a university near my parents. The general education classes were huge, and no one noticed if I attended or not. I felt tiny and lost in a huge wave of humanity so I stayed home and listened to music in my bedroom so I didn't feel lonely.

Dance was the only thing that made me feel alive. I wanted to become a dance instructor. I loved my dance classes until the day I attended a dance concert where my modern dance teacher acted out a rape scene on stage with her male partner. The dance was beautiful and powerful, depicting the change that happens in a young woman when violated. I had no idea why I reacted the way I did, but my dream of dancing immediately died, causing my downward plunge to steepen. I struggled to go to class, focus, or even leave my bedroom.

Mom enlisted the help of a highly recommended child psychologist, but he gave up after six months, saying there was something I was withholding and there was nothing more he could do.

So I ran away to a summer job at a resort in Jackson Hole, Wyoming. There were only two types of kids up there—the church kids and the partiers. There was no way I was going to hang out with the church kids. One gangster with bright-red glasses showed me how to roll joints and kept passing me beers until I'd downed half a dozen. He took me back to his room where he made it to second base before I wordlessly objected and he stopped. With no idea how to make a graceful exit, I lay awake in the dark until long after he'd fallen asleep. His roommate returned with a girl, and I listened to them having sex a few feet away. In the morning, I returned home a failure after only three days away.

I decided I needed to have fun, so I went to my first dance, where I met a handsome man who was an amazing dancer. I'd initiated the few dates I had in high school, so when Carson asked me out, I was thrilled. We hit it off, and a week later he asked me to come with him when he moved to California because he'd accepted a transfer to run his own arcade.

7

Since I loved the beach and wanted the opportunity to live life as an adult, the decision was easy. My family didn't like him, but I didn't care; their objections only drove me deeper into Carson's passionate arms.

Losing my virginity was confusing for me. When he whispered into my ear, "Are you sure you want this?" I quickly responded, "Yes." My words lit a fire within him that took control. But there was no matching fire inside of me; instead, I felt detached. When he was finished, I wanted to throw him off me and scream at him to get out of my house. I was angry and in pain. I didn't know where the feelings had come from or why they threatened to destroy me.

Though I felt Carson's love was suffocating me, I continued planning the wedding. Three months after we met, we were married in my parents' living room. That morning, I knew I was making the biggest mistake of my life, but I went through with it anyway. Two days later, we packed our few belongings and headed west.

The year and a half I lived with Carson was a blur of darkness and pain. I molded myself to be what he wanted while he kept me on a tight leash. I loved the ocean but wasn't allowed to go there. Carson let me go grocery shopping and to my part-time job in a department store by myself, but other than that, he needed to be with me to "protect me."

I never understood why he kicked me out three months into our marriage. He wanted to be single again, so Mom flew me home. Days later, Carson changed his mind and convinced me to return. I found out a year later that he'd tried to sleep with someone else while I was gone, which made him realize that he actually loved me. No matter how hard we tried, our relationship never improved. God spoke to me in the middle of a parking lot, warning me that if I stayed, he would destroy the tiny bit of myself I'd managed to hold on to.

I convinced Carson I was a horrible wife and that he deserved better. He agreed, and within days we told our families we were separating. I left the next week, before he could change his mind. I managed to resist his attempts to woo me back with promises of change only because bits of his true personality kept shining through his hollow words.

I don't know why I was terrified of him. He cheated on me, but I would have returned—if not for the terror. He'd put his fist through the wall and shattered a large picture of the two of us, but he kept his promise never to hit me. Yet, somehow, I knew if I went back, his promise would be broken.

Our do-it-yourself divorce was final in three months, without either of us having to show up in court. By then I had met another man. Chad wasn't as charismatic as Carson, but he was safe. He was also a devout Mormon. The chemistry wasn't there for me, but it was, again, a way out of my parents' house. I returned to church for him and embraced the Mormon lifestyle. We married within a year, and soon I was pregnant. I buried the past and focused on the future I was creating with my new husband.

While my siblings can talk for hours about their memories of our various homes, most of what they talk about is new to me. Yet it is through those conversations that I've been able to remember as much as I do, though I stumble onto black holes that cover vast stretches of time. I thought it was normal not to remember, normal to feel like my siblings grew up somewhere different from me, normal for childhood memories to be covered in darkness. I was wrong.

2

A BROKEN CHILD

I needed to find Michael. He'd been quiet for five minutes which meant disaster in some form or another. Michael was my best friend, Jessica's, child and I babysat him while she worked.

"I'll be right back," I said to my four-year-old son, Gavin. In response, he hit his head with his fist repeatedly. I wanted to stay and give Gavin the attention he needed, but I needed to find out what Michael had discovered to capture his short attention span. Gavin hit his head frequently when Michael was at our house, but I didn't know what to do about it, since my friend had no money to pay someone to watch her son.

I glanced into rooms on my way down the hall but didn't see anything until I got to my bedroom. Michael emerged from the attached bathroom, glanced at me, and hurried past—a definite sign of trouble. I continued into the bathroom and looked around. At the bottom of the deep, jetted tub I saw what he'd been playing with.

The Blackthorn Fairy figurine my mother brought back from her trip to England lay broken in the bottom of the tub. I stared without moving. I only had three prized possessions. A statue Michael had broken two weeks earlier, an antique doll I'd inherited from my mother, and the Blackthorn Fairy.

Mom had said when she saw this fairy, happy and skipping, it reminded her of me as a child. The fairy looked about the age I would have been in Colorado, the eighteen months that I considered my childhood. When we moved away I broke just like my little fairy.

I pushed down my emotions, gently picked up my figurine, and carried it out of the bathroom. It was my own fault for keeping the fairy on the tiled ledge on the far side of the tub. I didn't think Michael was big enough to climb in and out.

A few more minutes, I reminded myself as I walked back down the hall. Jessica would arrive soon to pick up Michael. I set the broken fairy on the small table near the front door and went into the kitchen where I'd left Gavin. In the minute or so I'd been gone, Michael had managed to climb up the shelves, grab two fruit snacks, and get back to the table where he munched happily while Gavin still struggled to open his treat. I was too tired to scold Michael.

The boys were opposites in appearance, though the same age. Michael was scrawny and towheaded while Gavin was built like a tank with deep chocolate skin. They attended the same early intervention preschool, Michael for speech, Gavin for mild attachment disorder. While the adoption papers claimed Gavin enjoyed a healthy pregnancy, I suspected he had fetal alcohol disorder due to the number of issues we'd already dealt with.

I sat down at the table while two little mouths devoured their gummy fruit. A moment of peace was all I'd get and I desperately needed it. Gavin was my youngest and tending Michael pushed me to the limit of what I could handle with four other children who had their own issues.

The doorbell rang and Michael jumped from his chair, the last gummy already in his mouth. I left Gavin to finish and walked into the adjoining living room where Michael had already pulled the door open for his mom.

I smiled at Jessica.

"That car sucks gas," Jessica blurted. "I just filled it and its already half empty." Jessica flung her long blonde hair over her shoulder and picked up her son. "I think there's something wrong with it."

When Jessica had left her husband with no car and no money, I'd offered to loan her the car we got for our oldest son, Ethan, who was close to getting his driver's license. "The repair shop fixed it up when we got it, but we haven't driven it much yet, so I don't know what kind of mileage it gets."

"Even my kids are embarrassed to ride in that car," Jessica complained. "They call it a hooptie and don't want any of their friends to see them in it."

The car was old, but that didn't mean they needed to call it a hooptie. I thought it looked great for its age. It was certainly better than not having a car. She'd shown a similar lack of gratitude when I'd helped gather items for her new apartment after she'd separated from her husband. She had commented that the mattress was hard, the bedding was a weird color, and she really needed a floor lamp instead of a table lamp. The items were from my mother, who was downsizing. I should have let her sleep on the floor a few nights before arranging for my parents to haul the items in their truck an hour and a half to her apartment. I looked away, shoved my thoughts down and returned my gaze to my friend.

"How was Michael today?" Jessica asked.

"He had fun, though he broke my fairy." I pointed to the happy fairy, both ankles broken and a bit of wire the only thing holding her upright at an odd angle.

"Oh, sorry," she said breezily. "I'll pay for it."

"My mother bought it in England, so I won't be able to replace it."

"Oh." She hitched Michael up higher on her hip as he cuddled into her neck. "Well, I better get going."

"Okay." We both knew she'd never pay me back and it wouldn't matter if she did, the item was irreplaceable. At least she'd sounded appropriately disturbed when Michael had pulled the statue of a mother and baby off the table where it crashed on the floor right in front of us, scattering bits and pieces. I had managed to glue it back together, but I did a bad job of it. The artistic beauty of the expensive statue would never be the same as when it was given to my husband and myself during my first pregnancy.

Jessica opened the door and retreated to her embarrassing car. I headed back to my bedroom to lay down, Gavin trailing behind me. He hated to have me out of his sight. He lined up his cars on the floor while I rested.

I tried to hold everything together, but I wasn't sure how much longer I could last. My husband, Chad, had begun his master's program in business only three months earlier. The chronic health problems I'd had since marrying Carson interfered with Chad's associate's degree, forcing him to drop his classes every time I got too sick to care for myself or our young children. Just before our tenth anniversary, he'd gone back to school to get his bachelor's degree. Our marriage barely survived, but Chad worked tirelessly to mend our relationship. What began as seeking safety had developed into the type of love I never believed existed. I needed to support him though this final push of school.

The yard had been torn up after a windstorm almost uprooted an eighty-foot tree with root rot forcing us to have it removed. Chad and I spent every spare moment we had trying to fix up the yard and build a retaining wall. Between the yard work, watching Michael, and tending my own kids, I was exhausted. I didn't mind the physical exhaustion; it was the mental depletion that left me feeling empty.

3

PARALYZED

A week later, my daughter, Nicole, played with her two younger siblings so I could get everything ready for her birthday party that afternoon. She had turned twelve earlier in the week and was excited to have her friends over. I'd spent a couple of hours cleaning and had almost forgotten to make the cake. I dumped ingredients into the mixing bowl and began beating it into a smooth batter.

Nicole and Gavin came up the stairs next to the kitchen. "Gavin wants an apple for a snack," she said as she headed to the table and grabbed an apple from the wooden basket there.

"Okay, thanks for helping him." I'd woken up with stiff muscles from too much yard work the day before. I wanted to get everything ready so I could rest.

Nicole cut the apple into slices on our stainless-steel countertop.

"Can I have caramel with my apple?" Gavin looked at me with hopeful eyes.

"We don't have any. Grandma was the one with the caramel dip." I pulled down two round cake pans and greased and floured them.

"I want to go to Grandma's house."

"Grandma doesn't live here anymore, Gavin," Amber interjected from the open stairwell. Amber was only seven but tall enough to fool people into thinking she was twelve. She certainly loved to poke holes into Gavin's happiness like a preteen.

"Why did Grandma move away?" Gavin pouted.

"Because she wanted to live in Logan," I said as I poured the batter into the pans.

"I hate Logan!"

"Gavin, here's your apple," Nicole said.

"I want dipping sauce!"

I debated what to do. If I said the wrong thing, a tantrum might last for five minutes or an hour. I didn't have an hour to spare.

"How about I sprinkle cinnamon on it? It's yummy," Nicole said. She was often my saving grace, quiet, helpful, and empathetic.

Ethan and Calvin would likely remain sequestered in their shared room to avoid being asked to do anything. Ethan only emerged to practice driving and eat while fourteen-year-old Calvin spent his hours designing and building inventions.

I slid the cake into the hot oven just as Amber said, "I want an apple."

Gavin happily accepted his cinnamon sprinkled apples and sat at the table while Nicole grabbed another apple for Amber.

"I'm tired, I'm going to lie down for a little while before the party," I said to the kids.

"Okay," Nicole said.

I slogged to my bed and flopped down on it. A prickly, cold sensation spread through the veins in my legs—an unusual sensation that only came with attacks of paralysis that I thought were a thing of the past.

Not again. The frequent paralytic attacks I'd experienced in my late twenties and early thirties had tapered off as I learned how to take better care of myself. I'd only had one attack in the last five years.

I needed to get into a comfortable position before it was too late. I tried to shift my leg, but it remained still. The paralysis was moving quickly—a bad sign.

Gavin wandered in. "Watcha doing, Mama?"

"Mommy needs to rest for a little while. I'm going to take a nap, okay?" I didn't want him to know what was happening. The older kids had been traumatized by these attacks when they were young.

"Okay." Gavin bounded out of the room, closing the door behind him. Gavin was my baby and, like the others, it had taken a miracle for him to come to our home. Ethan had been born nine weeks premature, Calvin had required months of bed rest, and Nicole's pregnancy had almost killed me. Surgery assured us there would be no more biological children, and I was happy with three. God had other plans, and we'd adopted Amber and Gavin.

I picked up the phone before my arms became useless, asking my next-door neighbor to come over. Then I called a friend to pick up the pizza for the party. Finally, as the heaviness crept up my arms, I dialed Chad's number.

"I'm having another attack. A bad one," I said. I wasn't going to be able to hide it like I had the last.

19

"I can leave right now, but I'm not sure what the train schedule is like this time of day. I don't how long it will take me to get home."

"I already called Jill. She just got here. I didn't want to be alone, just in case." I rested my arm on the pillow, keeping my cell phone cradled between my hand and cheek.

"I should still come home."

"No, Jill is here, the party is ready except for the pizza, and Livvy is picking that up for me. I need to go. I just wanted to let you know what was happening."

"Okay, thanks. I love you."

"I love you too."

I used the last of my strength to end the call and flopped my arm into a more comfortable position.

With nothing else to do but rest, I pictured the first time I saw Amber. Chad picked up the scrawny brown baby girl and held her in his arms. Born premature and addicted to cocaine, she had just gotten out of the hospital when we drove to Detroit to meet her. For Chad, it was love at first sight, but I was still mourning the loss of the child we were prepared to bring home only a week earlier before the birth mother had backed out.

Chad handed Amber to me, and I took the tiny two-week-old, barely five-pound baby girl into my arms. I knew there was no way I was going to leave her without a family, and I shoved down my fear of learning how to do black hair, of messing up as white parents raising a black child, and even the unknown of what the drugs might have done to her.

It took three months of red tape to bring her home, and a year later, the problems started cropping up. I fought the doctors for Amber to get the care she needed and learned to do without sleep. It was all difficult enough that I rejected the thought of adopting another baby despite our original plans to do so.

I fought the insistence of my heart that I needed to adopt again—until God blessed me with a vision of Gavin as a full-grown adult. At that moment, I experienced the full bloom of a mother's love for him. I had to find him and bring him home despite the numerous obstacles that stood in our way. I'll never forget the lonely drive through the rain-soaked streets of a strange city in the middle of the night to meet him. I was terrified that somehow it wouldn't be him. I picked him up, cradling another tiny baby in my arms, and looked into his eyes for the first time. It was my Gavin.

A familiar fuzziness crept into my thoughts as the attack progressed, and I welcomed the calm, timeless space my brain entered.

Every so often, Jill would peek in to check on me and make sure I was still conscious. I would answer her inane questions, wishing her and her discomfort away.

The worst of attacks could shut all my muscles down, even my lungs and heart. Worry managed to worm its way into that empty space in my brain, and so I focused all my energy and managed to cause the end of one finger to twitch. The motion comforted me. I was still breathing and conscious, both good signs.

The doorbell chimed, and footsteps echoed across the hard floors.

"I put the pizza on the counter in the kitchen," Livvy said from my doorway.

"Thank you. There's money in my wallet." The exertion of speaking stole my breath away. I took a couple of shallow breaths, then said, "It's in my purse. Maybe by the nightstand."

"I don't see it here, but don't worry about that. We'll settle up later."

My phone rang, so Livvy picked it up and held it to my ear.

"How are you?" Chad asked.

"Okay. I can still wiggle my middle finger a little, so I'll be fine."

"I called the doctor, and he said to eat some high-potassium foods. I don't think he understands what you are experiencing. I think you should have some Gatorade, though. That might help."

"Okay. Bye."

"Bye, honey."

Livvy moved the phone away from my ear and turned it off. "You need Gatorade. Where is it?"

It was nice to be taken care of for a change. "There should be some in the cupboard in the mudroom." Livvy's footsteps faded away.

When she returned, I forced my heavy eyelids open a crack to see a glass with orange liquid and a straw. I was only able to open my mouth and wait for her to move the straw into it.

I took a long sip, paused for breath, then took another sip. Too tired to continue, I said, "I'm done."

"I have kids in the car, so I have to go, but I'll check on you later."

"Okay. Thanks." *Please don't leave me.* Unfazed by my condition, she was a comforting presence. She turned and walked away.

The paralysis settled fully into my eyelids, and my breathing worsened. I wondered if I'd die right here, with Jill in the other room watching the kids.

Jill returned. "Is this the same color as the living room?" she asked, referring to the paint on my walls.

"No . . ." breath, "this . . ." breath, "is . . ." breath, "more . . ." breath, "gray."

Please don't ask me anything else. I'm too tired. Jill returned to the kids as if she'd heard my thoughts. I focused only on the battle of sucking in life and lost track of time.

Gradually, the air came easier. I relaxed, knowing that I'd eventually be fine. When the attacks hit, the paralysis crashed over my body like a wave hitting the shore. I never knew how far it would flow until the moment it receded, returning to wherever it came from.

I let myself float in timeless space until it too faded, bringing increasing brain function and awareness of my body. The annoying buzz in my crooked leg became almost unbearable due to my inability to move it into a more comfortable position.

My neck ached from being propped up in the same spot. To distract myself, I focused on the finger I'd twitched earlier until a tiny jerk left me feeling satisfied that I had some measure of control and wasn't completely trapped in my body.

With nothing else to do, I continued twitching my finger, resting in between each attempt, until I was able to jerk my fingers into a mechanical, clenching-type motion. Function was returning.

The next time Jill popped her head in, I said, "I'll be okay now. You can leave." I was happy to hear my voice sounding normal again.

"I'll just stay to make sure you're okay."

The positions of my kinked neck and crooked leg were unbearable. With enough energy in my core to keep from flopping like a dead fish, I opened my mouth. "Can you move my pillow out from under my head?"

23

Jill came over, and I mustered all my strength to lift my body and keep my head from hanging limply. She pulled the pillow away, and I sunk down, grateful to be able to rest without my neck hurting. I savored the feeling, choosing to focus on what I'd managed to accomplish rather than on the continued discomfort in my leg.

Resting there, my brain came fully online, and a sense of panic engulfed me. The last time the paralysis had moved into my lungs, I had lost consciousness and almost died. I was terrified of leaving my children without a mother.

An icy truth washed over me. I was powerless to keep the promise I'd made to my kids that my attacks were in the past. I assumed the lifestyle changes I'd made would keep them from returning, even though doctors hadn't been able to determine the cause. I wanted to believe my words as much as the kids did, but it was a lie.

Soon I was able to move my arms, then my legs, in reverse order from how the attack started. I shifted in bed, then was able to sit up. I sent Jill home.

When I was able to walk again, I resumed getting ready for the party. I smiled and pretended I was fine. Hopefully, the kids had no idea what happened. No one except Chad knew about my attack a year ago, and no one needed to know now.

The party was in full swing by the time Chad got home. He looked worried, so I put him to work frosting the cake. I stayed quiet.

Doctors wanted answers. If I went to them, they would order expensive tests and send me to specialists who would either throw possible diagnoses and treatments at me or decide I was crazy. That was what had happened when my attacks started at age twenty-six. One thing we knew was that overworking my muscles played the biggest role in the attacks, and so Chad banned me from working in the yard. I didn't object.

The fatigue lingered, which was unusual, but I assumed I'd pushed my body hard enough I'd used up my stores of energy and needed a prolonged rest. I assured Chad I was fine and worked to show him it was true. Another lie. The next attack came two days later.

4

CHANGE OF PLANS

The loss of control over my body was devastating. The attacks didn't follow a pattern; they came at different times of day, with various levels of intensity, and lasted one to two hours.

I pretended to be fine and that it didn't bother me, but deep down I feared I could die at any moment without ever having known what it was like to live. I'd put off my dreams to raise my children, pretending that my future was guaranteed. I wanted to travel and see the places I saw in pictures. Even if I didn't die, I wondered if it would be safe to travel when I could collapse at any moment.

Would the attacks continue for months, years, or longer? I tried to tell myself they would stop, that this was just a hiccup in my life and I could be the mother I always wanted to be. My fear didn't subside; neither did the attacks.

While these attacks resembled the previous ones, there were distinct differences—they lasted longer and drained me of energy for days. Where I had bounced back between attacks when I was younger, now my muscles became weakened with a fatigue that left little energy for simple things, like walking.

I managed to get around the house most days, but shopping was beyond my capacity. I became homebound and unable to participate in any of my normal activities, like going to church.

But I was determined to fight back. Rather than wallow in helplessness, I reached out to a neighbor who had a spare wheel-chair in her garage. It didn't have a seat cushion and was way too small for my tall frame, but at least I could get around with it.

I used it for the first time the next day in church. I had missed three weeks and was eager to return to my community of friends.

Chad put a red sofa pillow on the seat and lifted the heavy wheelchair in and out of the van. It hurt my sense of fashion and independence, but I pasted on a smile.

Determined to regain some control, I insisted on pushing myself into the building, but there was a gentle incline up to the door that was too much for my weakened muscles. "It's too steep. I can't do it," I told Chad, who was right behind me and stepped forward to push me into the church.

"I'll push myself now that it's level." I began rolling across the thin industrial carpet, surprised at how difficult it was. But I refused to give in and slowly pushed myself, though I was winded and exhausted by the time I got to the back of the chapel.

My friends and fellow congregants peppered me with questions. I gave rote answers with a huge smile. "My attacks of paralysis have returned, but I'm fine," I lied. In only three weeks, my body had gone from being able to carry sixty-pound blocks of concrete in our backyard to barely being able to push myself in a wheelchair.

At the time, Mormons spent three hours in church every week. After the first hour, my back and hips ached. During the second hour, I got so cold in the air conditioning that I wondered if I'd ever get warm again. By the end of the third hour, I was exhausted, miserable, and wanted nothing more than to climb into bed. Despite all of that, I was happy to be out of the house and enjoyed the attention.

With little choice, I adapted to my new situation. My calves hurt when they got cold, so I took blankets to church until I discovered cute leg warmers on the internet. As my arms got weaker, I allowed Chad to push me on any surface that wasn't level and hard. Gradually, I lost control of every aspect of my life as the attacks kept coming. None of the things that had previously helped reduce the attacks were working this time.

I turned my assistive devices into friends by naming each one. My borrowed wheelchair was Billy since he was blue. Grandma's sparkly maroon walker became Edna. Edna had large wheels and a soft seat for carrying things or resting when I got too tired to walk.

My doctor referred me to the University of Utah Clinical Neurosciences Center, where I hoped the advances in medicine could give me a quick solution and treatment plan. While I waited for an appointment, I spent most of my days in bed, too weak to do housework or care for my children.

My muscles tired in walking the thirty feet from my bedroom to the kitchen. Initially, I would rest in a chair before I made the trek back to bed, but then I learned that by shifting my body back and forth, I could swing my legs around, using different muscles for the return trip. I didn't care if it looked ridiculous; it got me from one place to another. When even that was too much, I had my wheelchair or walker.

But then my arms weakened enough that I struggled to push myself in the wheelchair and had to rely on the kids to do it for me. Mom offered Grandpa's old Jazzy electric wheelchair. We brought the ugly thing home. I hated it; hated that I needed it. All my assistive devices were hand-me-downs, reminding me of my childhood. I needed to make this chair my own, so I painted flowers and swirls across the back and down the sides and named her Beulah.

Trips to the grocery store required I take the kids with me. One would push the cart and reach for the items that were too high for me, and another would push me in my wheelchair. Ethan, normally mature and responsible, would lose focus and run me into displays. Calvin pushed me like he was running the Daytona 500, which made me motion sick. Amber and Gavin were too young to push me straight, which meant my best option was Nicole. My life was full of finding the best person to help me with whatever I couldn't do on my own.

One day, the kids and I went to Costco to stock up on groceries —only to realize we'd left the wheelchair at home. I wanted to turn around and go home, but Ethan piped up. "They have wheelchairs here. I'll go get one for you."

I waited in the late summer heat while he went inside. He returned with a wheelchair that looked like it was built for a bear rather than a slim woman. I sat down. As Ethan pushed me and Nicole held Gavin's hand, an older man approached us.

"It looks like you're just faking it to get a ride out of your kids."

A chill swept over me, but I merely replied, "I wish."

From that moment on, I refused to go anywhere without my own wheelchair and desperately wished for a real wheelchair to show people I was disabled and wasn't faking.

As the weeks passed, I decided I better get some flats since the high-heels from my healthy days made the wheelchair even more uncomfortable.

On one of my strong days, Chad drove me to the shoe store. Gavin went everywhere with us, so while I rolled my chair over to look at shoes, Chad focused on keeping Gavin occupied. I headed down the first narrow aisle, but the shoes were high and out of sight. I looked at the tiny black-and-white pictures on the boxes, but they were no help.

I blindly reached up and touched the toe of the shoe above my head. I couldn't get a good enough grip to pull it down, but I managed to push the toe down so that the back of the shoe tipped up to where I could see it. I slowly went down the aisle, tipping each shoe for a glimpse and stopping frequently to rest my arm.

Eventually I found a pair of comfortable flats, but the tiny errand had exhausted me and had taken at least three times as long as it might have before the wheelchair. This was my new normal. Despite clinging to any bit of independence I could achieve, I didn't truly have any.

People were rushing from one thing to another while I sat back and watched. When I was out in public, I was either ignored or stared at. When I tried to get through crowded spaces, the tall people around me were oblivious to my presence, as if I were invisible so far below their line of sight.

Eventually, my mental health slipped, and I withdrew from everyone, even Chad. No one understood what it was like to have their life suddenly stolen away by the betrayal of their body. For hours I had nothing except my mind to keep me company, and I was afraid of the dark thoughts that resided there. I began binge-watching television, which did little to help my mental state.

Three months later, Chad took me to my first appointment with Dr. Smith, a neuromuscular specialist who turned out to be young enough to be up on current medicine but old enough to know what he was doing. My hopes soared.

"I read over your file. I want you to tell me everything from beginning to end, as if we have all the time in the world."

"Where do you want me to start?"

"When did you have your first attack?"

"I was twenty-six."

"Start by telling me about that attack and go forward from there. Tell me everything you can think of, and then I'll ask you some questions."

I began talking about the first terrifying attack that had landed me in the emergency room while Dr. Smith settled into typing everything into the computer.

"It took every bit of effort I had to breathe; I felt like an anvil was resting on my chest. I knew I was at a critical point, but I wasn't worried about it. I was a passive observer, knowing I would either stop breathing and be in real trouble or my next breath would come and I'd eventually be fine. The next breath came. A few minutes later, I became aware of my surroundings again."

He didn't interrupt and tell me I wasn't unconscious or look at me like I was crazy when I talked about that dark place inside me where I go. He didn't even contradict me about it being difficult to breathe. Doctors rarely believed me.

"At the hospital, I began coming out of the attack. They ran tests but found nothing. I kept having attacks for the next five years but never as bad as the first. I saw a bunch of specialists, who ran tons of tests, but they never found a cause. The neurologist wrote that I had periodic paralysis but decided it was caused by anxiety, so I stopped going to doctors."

"And then they stopped?" he clarified.

"Yeah, they gradually tapered off as I learned to take better care of myself, then stopped completely.

"What did you do to take better care of yourself that seemed to help?"

"I don't push my body. I found out I had Hashimoto's thyroiditis and have kept a careful eye on my TSH levels, and if I get sick, I rest. Those things seemed to help."

"No changes to your diet?"

"Not really. I eat pretty healthy most of the time, though."

"Anything else?"

"Last year I had an attack, along with some heart palpitations. I did a stress test, and the cardiologist started me on potassium pills, which seemed to unlock my energy. I did great until my attacks started up again."

"You need a genetic test to make sure, but everything you've told me matches with hypokalemic periodic paralysis. I feel comfortable getting you started on potassium packets. When you have an attack, you need large amounts of potassium to stop them.

"There is a list of possible symptoms, but not everyone experiences the same symptoms. Stress makes it worse, as well as overworking your muscles. Your food journal looks pretty good; I don't see any problems that jump out there."

I headed home with high hopes. I just knew I would be out of the wheelchair and back on my feet soon.

The orange-flavored packets of potassium I added to my water tasted horrible. They seemed to help a little, but not much. The attacks kept coming, and I continued to weaken.

A month later, I went in for a follow-up appointment. My muscle tests showed my muscles were strong but had no endurance. Dr. Smith had no answers as to why I was too weak to walk.

"This borrowed wheelchair is making things worse," I complained. "My back and hips hurt within ten minutes."

"I can order you a custom ultralight wheelchair and at least fix that problem."

"Am I going to use it enough to need my own?"

Dr. Smith sat back and folded his arms. "There's no way I can tell you one way or another. There's too much we don't know. Some people have attacks that come in cycles, like yours; they will have a bunch and then stop for a while. If I had to guess, I'd say you will most likely be in and out of a wheelchair the rest of your life. Once people with hypokalemic periodic paralysis start using a wheelchair, they tend to continue to need one because the attacks damage muscle over time. My best guess is that you'll never go longer than a couple of years without needing a wheelchair."

My heart sunk, but it made the choice easy. "Okay, let's order one then. I just need to get it on my insurance this year before my coverage changes in January."

"It will be tough, but we'll try to get it before the year is out." He wrote the order, and we headed back to our van.

I sat stoically while my emotions warred within me. I was excited to be more comfortable and that others would know I had a legitimate health issue, but devastation swept over me as the future I'd waited for disappeared. As Chad wheeled me to the car, I thought of my dream of going to Hawaii. Over the years,

I'd fleshed out the details: I'd walk along the pristine beaches, my toes squishing into the soft sand. The air would be full of the foreign smells of flowers and plants. I'd hike into the mountains and feel the spiritual energy of mana connecting me to the uniqueness of the land and culture.

At the car, I shifted into my seat. Chad rolled the wheelchair to the back of the van and put it away. I stared at my hands as he started the car and drove out of the parking garage.

I looked out the window, imagining the trip to Hawaii. I saw Chad carrying me across the sand and laying me on a beach chair. He sat beside me, staying with me rather than enjoying the beach or water. We watched others walk, splash, and surf. I said, "I'm hot, can we go back?" I wasn't hot, but I couldn't bear to watch everyone else enjoying the vacation I wanted to have. I pictured us touring the island by rental car instead. It was lovely but not the dream I'd carried in my heart for years.

I consoled myself with a sigh, knowing reality rarely measured up to dreams anyway.

"You okay?" Chad asked.

"Yeah. It's just tough to hear I'll be in and out of a wheelchair the rest of my life."

A heavy silence descended. I was thirty-nine and my life was over.

At home the depression settled over me like a heavy blanket, blocking me from a world that raced ahead without me. I stayed cheerful around my children, but when they were gone or asleep, I grieved.

The day arrived to be measured for my wheelchair. Chad rolled me into a small shop cluttered with wheelchairs and sample books. My eyes were drawn to a light-blue chair with a rigid frame. It looked like a proper wheelchair, not something anyone could get off Amazon.

"There is a benefit to transporting a collapsible wheelchair, but the rigid frame has detachable parts that would make it lightweight enough for you to lift easier," the salesman said as he pointed to the examples.

He leaned down and removed the wheel of the light-blue wheelchair in one quick motion, showing me how easy it was. "The wheels are the heaviest part of the chair, weighing five pounds each. Once you take those off, the frame is much lighter."

I needed as much independence as possible. "That's what I want."

"Okay. Let's get your measurements. This chair will be built according to the measurements we give them."

He alternately measured the various lengths of my body and wrote notes on his clipboard. "Now you get to choose the color." He held out one of the sample books; it had squares of color marching across the page in neat lines.

My eyes scanned past the neon and animal prints to settle on a color that lit me with happiness. I pointed to a sparkly, deep purple. "That's what I want."

"Okay." He made another notation on his clipboard. "I like your decisiveness."

A few more decisions and we were on our way. It wasn't until later that I understood the significance of the color I had been drawn to.

#memory

It was July, and my seventh birthday was only a month away. I wanted a bike more than anything. A bike represented freedom and the ability to travel farther from home. In Colorado, my family wasn't yet destitute, but we didn't have much left over either. I had accidentally seen the ugly light-yellow bike, its banana seat split down the center. It gave me time to adjust so I would be happy when Dad wheeled it out.

I waited impatiently for my birthday to come so I could start riding my ugly bike around. Kids might make fun of me, but I didn't care. Mom might even let me ride my bike to my best friend, Katie's, house.

The day arrived, and I excitedly went out to the driveway so Dad could deliver my present. He emerged not with the chipped yellow paint and split seat but with a beautiful purple bike that sparkled in the sun and sported a shiny new black seat. It was love at first sight. My eyes drank it in, and I stepped over the elegantly curved frame to test out the height so Dad could adjust the seat.

"What happened to the yellow bike?" I asked.

"This is the yellow bike," Dad replied. "Tim helped me strip off all the paint, and we repainted it and got a new seat."

I looked at my new bike with even more astonishment. How could this beautiful bike have come from all that ugliness?

It was the first time I realized Dad loved me; otherwise, why would he have spent so much time fixing up that old bike?

My brother taught me how to ride it that afternoon, and a whole new world opened up. My bike represented growing up, being independent, feeling loved, and receiving something I desperately wanted, which rarely happened.

Weeks later, my sparkly purple wheelchair arrived. I sank into the cushions and propelled myself smoothly across the hardwood floors of my house like a cloud floating with the breeze. I named my wheelchair Veronica, and I loved her. She and I glided though stores, and people treated me differently, like I knew they would. I let go of my dreams and accepted the task of building a life around my new limitations. My only other choice was to lie in bed and waste away. My children still needed their mother, so I fought for them by fighting for myself.

5

LOSS

Jessica was my best friend—the first I'd had since Katie in the third grade. I'd provided emotional support in addition to loaning her the car and giving her things to outfit her apartment. She promised over and over that she'd always be there for me when I needed her. Everything changed when my health declined.

Jessica had always been abrasive and outspoken, but she was young and fun, so it never bothered me before. She got irritated that I couldn't babysit her son any longer, which I had always done for free. She complained about my wheelchair as if I was purposely trying to annoy her with this change in my life. One day, I'd complained over the phone about my new situation for several minutes before saying, "I don't even want to go out anymore. It's too hard."

"You know, Barb has the same condition and yet she comes to church every Sunday with a smile on her face and never complains."

I was stunned. Words came out of my mouth to end the call, but I wasn't paying attention to what they were.

I'd listened to hours of Jessica complaining about everyone around her, her situation, and her children. She hadn't been able to listen to five minutes of the struggles I needed to vent about. Not only that, but Barb didn't have periodic paralysis; she had multiple sclerosis. Barb was amazing, with a peace and beauty to her soul that touched everyone around her. Comparing myself to her, I came up woefully short.

I stopped complaining, instead shoving everything down. I pasted a smile on no matter what. If I was too tired to do that, I stayed home in bed.

My depression became worse again, and the anxiety I'd struggled with throughout my life increased dramatically. Things deteriorated with Jessica until every conversation hurt. Misunderstandings multiplied until our relationship disintegrated as quickly as it had come, leaving me bitter.

As I lay in my bed, too tired to even get up to do the dishes, I realized I'd been duped. I'd given Jessica everything I had at the expense of my family, and she had been happy to take it all.

I stared at the ceiling and thought of all I had lost. Her son had broken the few prized possessions I owned, and I'd frankly forgiven him. Never had Jessica tried to make up for it in any way.

All along she'd bled me dry, giving only little bits in return. I thought it was because she had little money, but now I knew that she had never truly been my friend. She disappeared into her new life, and I was left alone. Again.

It was my fault, as usual. I had a pattern of opening up quickly, desperate for friendship, and then discovering that others only wanted to take. I'd been doing it my whole life. I'd thought

Jessica was different. We'd been friends for over a year, with me trusting her, and she had hurt me worse than all the rest of my so-called friendships combined.

I wallowed in bed all day long, feeling too weak to do anything. The next day I used what little energy I had to get ready for church.

I sat through the long talks. Chad wheeled me to Sunday School, where Barb sat in her wheelchair on one side, I in mine on the other, at the edges of the room. There was no room for us anywhere else. Being with the others didn't bother me when Chad sat beside me, but after Sunday School, the women remained in the room for a lesson while the men congregated in a different room for their own lesson.

I sat and listened to the other women talk as they waited. Looking over, I saw them in groups of twos, threes, and fours. There were smiles, laughter, and togetherness emanating from them, but no one sat by me. Even Barb had someone beside her; she always did. The minutes ticked slowly by as I sat alone.

It had taken me years to be brave enough to sit by someone else, but I'd worked on it so I wouldn't have to sit alone and go unnoticed. I'd sat next to different people until eventually I'd become friendly with most of the church ladies.

Now, as I sat there watching the groups of women chatting amongst themselves, I reminded myself I wasn't always alone. Often, the older ladies would sit by me, and they always checked to see how I was doing. We had similar complaints and ailments, which gave us something to talk about. Today that didn't help. Today, when I needed someone so desperately, I sat alone. I wanted to roll out of the room to get away, but my weakness had me trapped.

Despite these struggles, I tried to prove my faith to God by continuing to go to church as often as I was able. Women my age or younger were extremely uncomfortable around me. They tried to hide it, but it rolled off them in waves, so they avoided me.

I wasn't prepared for the isolation that accompanied my health limitations. I stayed away from the awkwardness of strangers, expecting the friends I thought I'd made and my family to rally around me, but they were busy with their lives. It reminded me of my childhood.

At age ten I got a head cold. One of my brothers had built a shelf and hung it on the wall above his bed for his boom box and speakers. He had set it up so when he lay in bed, he had perfect stereo sound.

I slathered Vicks on my chest to help me breathe and went to his room. I popped a tape into the player and snuggled into his cozy bed. The music played in my head with perfect stereo sound, lulling me into a much-needed sleep. When I woke up, I crept out of his room, making sure to put everything back in place so I wouldn't get in trouble. I never thought about the smell of the Vicks.

He yelled with enough frustration I never did it again. He didn't care that I was sick and his room made me feel better. Both my oldest brothers treated me like an annoying fly. I was young and stupid back then, and now, compared to their perfect scores and high-tech jobs, I hadn't changed much.

Next oldest was Rick, the typical older brother, who teased me incessantly and sat on me until I consented to be his slave for the day, which generally consisted of changing the three channels on the box television before remotes were invented. As an adult, I drove up to visit Rick and his family more often than anyone else, but I rarely spent much time there. I enjoyed the quiet away from the city, but farming took most of Rick's time.

My only sister, Marie, came after Rick. "Tumultuous" is the best word to describe our relationship as kids. She was bossy and told me I was spineless. I ignored her and became a tomboy. It got much better when Marie needed a place to live for a month while I was having my first set of attacks. She helped around the house, and we began getting along, though we still went months between phone calls. In my family, that was considered close.

Dave was the only one younger than I was. We both longed for deeper family connection and stayed close, but over the years as our lives diverged, we gradually talked less.

Years ago, I started a family newsletter and hounded my siblings for information about what was going on until I got tired and busy. I stopped, and no one cared enough to take it up again. The only other person beside Marie that I bothered to keep in contact with was Mom.

Mom had rheumatic fever when she was a kid, and understanding what it felt like to suffer, she always took good care of anyone who was sick or struggling. Mom was a workaholic, choosing work over the stress of family life. For years I told my kids they would know Grandma was coming if the doorbell rang and she was on the other side of the door, since most of the time she rescheduled or canceled.

Now that I was sick, it was my turn for Mom's love and attention, even though she lived an hour and a half away. Once a week, she would stop in after she finished work in Salt Lake

City and clean my house. Then she'd stay overnight at her sister's house, work another day in Salt Lake, then travel home and work remotely the rest of the week. I loved the attention she gave me. Those evenings were the highlight of my week. The kids loved being with their grandma as much as I loved it.

Most of my in-laws lived nearby but rarely visited or offered to help. My mother-in-law called every month or so to see how I was doing but kept herself busy helping her daughters. When I was strong enough to get up the stairs into her house, I went for Sunday dinner, but most of the time I stayed home. I kept quiet about my loneliness, my dirty house, and my suffering family. I was never comfortable around my in-laws, and over time, their discomfort with me grew. Now I was in a wheelchair, which made most people uncomfortable around me anyway.

In my wheelchair, I generally sat at the edges of rooms and gatherings. Having to navigate through chairs, purse straps on the floor, and other obstacles kept me wherever I was placed.

One time, Chad's family wanted to meet at a restaurant for dinner. I was placed at the far end of the table and had to struggle to get there, disrupting strangers trying to enjoy their meals. Chad and I occupied the end together, leaving barely enough room for my plate at a table that didn't allow me to get close enough to eat easily.

I sat there, exhausted from the effort, struggling to get the food from the plate to my mouth, and listened to the happy conversations around me.

They began talking about training for marathons, something shared by many at the table. Conversation drifted from dietary restrictions and training schedules to how they felt about the training. I wanted to scream at them to stop talking about

44

marathons when I couldn't even walk to my kitchen, but as usual, I stayed silent.

I had to get out of there. I was physically exhausted, so I used that as my excuse. As soon as Chad took care of the check, we said goodbye.

"You're leaving already?" one sister exclaimed.

"Yes, I'm not feeling good." It was my standard response because it covered physical weakness, mental stress, actual sickness, or whatever else I needed it to. It was a net that caught everything because I never felt good. I preferred being home, where I was less lonely and felt somewhat normal, even though I averaged twenty-two hours per day in bed. People treated me differently now that I looked like a frail old lady hunched over in a wheelchair, but I was the same person inside.

Other than Mom's weekly visits, a few calls from my mother-in-law, and the ladies from church bringing meals from time to time, we were on our own physically and emotionally.

I used online shopping, even finding a new business that offered a grocery shopping service, something rare at the time. I arrived at the designated stop, they loaded the groceries into my van for me, and I drove home.

One day I felt strong enough to go into one of the smaller grocery stores for bread and milk with Gavin. I parked, and we headed in. Gavin climbed into the front of a cart that looked like a truck, and I shuffled to the far corner of the store for the milk. Halfway there, my legs began to weaken.

By the time I got to the dairy case, I knew I had to get out as soon as possible because this wasn't the usual weakness. It was an attack. One of my greatest fears was having another attack in public. In Wisconsin, my legs dropped me to the floor in the middle of the hallway at church. Congregants and leaders tried to help, but there was nothing to do but wait. I imagined myself splayed out on the cold linoleum floor, making everyone uncomfortable as I waited for an ambulance I couldn't afford to take me to the hospital where staff would stand about helplessly trying to figure out what to do for me.

I inched my way to the front of the store, splayed across my cart for support, to the checkout. I surrendered my cart and white-knuckled it along the tiny counter between the clerk and me to keep from falling. I paid for my milk and shuffled to the van, my son still pretending to drive from inside the cart.

Each movement drained my muscles, and I wasn't able to take the cart to the designated return. I silently apologized to the car that might want to park in the spot next to me and to the attendant who would have to retrieve the cart and guiltily got in my vehicle.

I only had to drive five minutes to get home. If I waited, Gavin and I would be stuck in the van for at least an hour. I started the car and maneuvered out of the lot. I weaved through the back streets where there was little traffic, just in case my brain wasn't as fit as I thought it was.

I started up a hill, but the muscles in my legs couldn't push the gas pedal any harder. The van slowed, needing more gas, so I pulled to the side of the road to rest. I sat there, talking to Gavin to keep us both calm, while fear pricked at my senses. If my muscles were too weak to hit the gas, they were too weak to hit the brakes. I was a danger to myself, my child, and others on the road.

I pushed down the anxiety, instead focusing on resting enough to get home. Half an hour later, I continued my trek.

The gas pedal felt like pushing weights, but I made it. I texted my son Ethan to bring the electric chair out. With Ethan homeschooled, there was always someone to help if I needed it. I'd also insisted Chad build a ramp since every entrance to the house had stairs.

I pulled into the garage, and Ethan stopped the chair several feet away to allow the van door to open. I swung my legs out and grabbed the door with one hand and the van frame with the other to pull myself up with my arms. But instead of standing, I collapsed onto the cold concrete. Ethan grabbed an arm to pull me up, but he was no match for my weight. I was cold, scared, and wanted my bed.

"Hook your arms under my shoulders and pull," I said. I summoned Herculean strength from deep inside and with Ethan's assistance managed to get into the chair. Ethan took care of Gavin and the milk while I manipulated the joystick to drive up the ramp and into my bedroom. Once there, I fell forward and used my momentum to roll myself onto the bed. I pulled a blanket over my body and shivered in an exhausted heap. Ethan brought another blanket and got Gavin settled while I lay helpless. It took another hour for the full attack to pass, but at least I had made it home and Gavin was safe.

I voluntarily stopped driving rather than risk an accident or having my driver's license revoked. My kids adapted. Calvin took a bus and train to his charter school, Nicole walked to junior high, Amber rode with a neighbor to her elementary school, and we requested a bus to take Gavin to preschool.

Amber and Gavin had special needs that required a healthy, full-time mom. Not being able to care for my children while they begged me to from the side of my bed tore at my heart.

One afternoon, I heard Gavin fighting with Amber in the basement yet could do nothing to intervene. Their yelling escalated, and soon Gavin ran up the stairs in tears. I had enough strength to lay my hand on his curly black hair and say, "What happened?"

"Amber's being mean to me!"

"I'm sorry. Do you want to sit with me for a minute?" I continued to stroke his hair.

"No! I want ramen."

"Okay. See if Nicole can make you some."

Gavin jerked away from my hand and stood defiantly. "No! I want you to do it."

"I can't, sweetie. I'm not feeling good. Go ask one of your brothers or Nicole to help you."

"They won't help me."

"Yes, they will. Go ask."

Gavin scampered away only to return less than a minute later with tears in his eyes. "Ethan's door is locked, and Nicole won't help me!"

"Go get Nicole for me."

Gavin left again, and I sighed. My kids were the most important thing in my life, but having five kids stretched me thin long before I became incapacitated. I wanted to roll over and shut everyone and everything out. I wanted to wallow in my pain without the demands of children, but I had no choice. I was the only mother they had.

Nicole came up the stairs and appeared in my doorway. "I'm in the middle of homework. I told him to ask Ethan."

"Gavin, did you knock on the door to ask Ethan and Calvin?"

"Calvin isn't home from school yet," Nicole said. She turned and left.

"Ethan won't do it!" Gavin yelled.

"Run and ask."

Gavin disappeared and returned even more distraught. "I told you he won't do it!" Gavin picked up a shoe and threw it across the room. His behavior—a cry for attention and help—was getting worse. Nicole appeared in the door.

"Nicole, will you please make him some ramen?"

"Come on, Gavin," she said.

I hated relying on Nicole so much, but I had no choice. I rolled over and let myself grieve in silence for a moment before stuffing my feelings down into the dark pit inside me where they wouldn't hurt me anymore.

6

DYING

I was failing as a mother. Chad got up early for the long commute to his job and stayed up late writing papers for his
classes. He did all he could to take care of me and the kids,
but there were only twenty-four hours in a day. I shopped for
Christmas presents online and enlisted Nicole to wrap them,
but I was basically helpless for anything else.

With Christmas vacation looming and my fatigue wors-
ening, I dreaded being helpless while the kids fought all day
without proper supervision. I picked up the phone and called
Mom.

"Hello?"

Tears choked my words. "Mom, I can't do this."

"Why? What's going on?"

"Whenever Amber and Gavin are home together, they
fight. And Gavin doesn't understand why I can't help him and
gets mad at me."

I swiped at the moisture on my face. "Why would God do this to me? He knew I would get sick and still gave me two kids that were hard even when I was healthy."

"I don't know, sweetie."

"These kids deserve a better parent. They already lost their birth parents; God should have given them to someone who could give them everything they need."

"Are you thinking about removing them from your home?"

"No. I don't want anyone else raising my kids. I just want to be healthy enough that I can do it myself." I'd lost too much already; I couldn't lose my kids too.

"Well, you aren't healthy enough. You need to think about the kids right now and what they need. I think I need to retire and bring the kids up here until you are stronger. You need to rest so you can get better."

"I've failed my kids. I hate knowing that, but what else can I do? I can't take care of them."

"You haven't failed; you are making sure your kids are taken care of."

With Mom, the kids would be gone only temporarily. It would be hard having them far away, but at least they would still be mine. I hated the thought of things getting bad enough that my kids were taken away because they got hurt without me there to watch over them or the state thought we were neglecting them. I couldn't let that happen.

"You only have one spare room, and these kids fight whenever they are together. Separate, they are fine, but no one can handle them both. Besides, I can't take Amber out of school. She's behind as it is. She hides in the basement and watches television from the moment she gets home and almost never talks to me. It's like she's afraid of me or that if she ignores me this will go away, but maybe with Gavin gone, I can help her."

"Dawn, you're too sick to take care of that little girl, and it sounds like she's struggling as much as Gavin is. You need to let the family help you. What about sending Amber to live with Rick and Jen? They have plenty of space, and Amber would have their two daughters to go to school with, so she won't feel so lost. Do you want me to talk to Jen about it?"

"No, I'll call her." I had no idea how I would do it, but Mom was right. I needed to think about the kids. I'd tried to get some help locally, but nothing had worked. I was out of options, and I didn't want to hurt my kids any more than they were already hurt.

"Do you want me to pick up Gavin after Christmas, or do you need me to come down and get him now?"

"Can you get him now?"

"Let me make some phone calls and work some things out. I'll come down tomorrow and pick him up, and then we'll bring him back for Christmas."

"Okay. That sounds good."

I called my brother's wife, Jen, and was shocked that she'd been thinking about the kids living with her when she'd seen how sick and weak I had been at Thanksgiving. She readily agreed to take Amber just after Christmas.

Relief swept over me as a huge burden was lifted, but I felt guilty. No good mother would be relieved her young children were moving away to two different cities, with the closest over an hour away.

Gavin left, and the constant strain was eased. It was only a week until Christmas, but it allowed us to get ready and for me to rest enough I could enjoy the holiday. He returned on Christmas Eve, happy and full of energy. The next day, he and Amber left with a few of their belongings in the small bags they had, the rest in garbage bags like foster kids I saw on television.

With my two youngest children cared for, the stress ebbed away. Chad figured out that massage helped me, so he got a massage table to work on bringing more oxygen to my muscles. I spent my days in bed, watching television and playing games on my phone, unable to focus enough to read, unable to hold my arms up to place pieces into my jigsaw puzzles.

My speech slowed, and thinking became difficult. Phone conversations made my head hurt within minutes. Simple words became lost in the abyss of my mind.

My shower chair helped me stay clean, but some days I was too weak to make the attempt. Fatigue settled over me like a weighted blanket, every movement a struggle against some unseen pressure. I focused on day-to-day survival.

One day, lying in bed with my eyes closed, I knew I needed to get up and go to the bathroom. I'd put it off long enough. I pushed my blanket aside, sat up, and slowly swung my legs off the side of the bed. I sat hunched over in my weary state until I had enough energy for the next step. My wheelchair sat parallel to the bed. I ignored my fatigue and managed to get into my chair.

I knew I wouldn't be able to rest until I was finished and back in bed, so I unlocked the wheels and pushed myself around the edge of the bed to the bathroom.

The chair didn't fit through either bathroom door, so I used the small en-suite bathroom because I could use the edge of the jetted tub on one side and the low counter opposite to support my weight, then get myself turned around and seated on the toilet, a few feet from the door.

I turned the wheelchair so I faced the bathroom and wedged it as far as it would go into the doorway. The toilet might as well have been a mile away. My body wasn't going to bridge the short distance. I had used all the strength I possessed to get from my bed to the bathroom.

I sat there and stared helplessly at the toilet; it would take too much energy to go forward, too much energy to go backward.

"Chad!" I yelled weakly.

The bedroom door was shut, and the normal sounds of living drowned out my voice. It was a Saturday, so I knew he was out there somewhere. "Chad!" Helpless and trapped, I called out once more.

Before I could figure out what to do or how to get enough energy to make it into the bathroom, Chad's firm steps sounded in the hall and the door opened. He turned and opened his drawer.

"Chad." He looked at me.

"I need help," I said, grateful an attack hadn't slid me out of my wheelchair and onto the floor.

"What do you need?"

"I don't have enough energy to go to the bathroom."

Without another word, Chad came over, pulled the chair out of the doorway, stepped through, then pulled it back into place. He hooked his arms under my armpits and lifted me up.

My legs barely supported me; my arms refused to move. "I can't do it."

Chad shifted to support me with his body and one arm while pulling down my pants and underwear. He then set me down on the toilet. I hope someday I will forget what it felt like to be hanging limply off my husband's body while he took care of me as if I were an infant.

He handed me the toilet paper, and I managed to take care of that part before he lifted me up, pulled my clothes into place, and gently set me in the wheelchair.

He pushed my wheelchair out, rolled me over to the bed, and lifted me into place.

"Do you need anything else?" he asked softly as he flipped the blanket over me.

"No, I just need to rest now."

"Okay."

He strode over to the dresser, picked up whatever it was he had been hunting for in the drawer, then left, closing the door quietly behind him.

I realized I hadn't washed my hands. I always washed my hands, more often than necessary. I wasn't clean. The agony settled deep in my heart at this new low. I couldn't even go to the bathroom by myself anymore. I couldn't do something as simple as wash my hands. I was a thirty-nine-year-old invalid.

I lay there exhausted, feeling death creep along my veins, sucking the life from my muscles. I had to face the truth. I was dying.

I'd been fighting it, and I began wondering why. I was a burden on my husband, who had given me everything, and yet I had nothing to give in return. I'd failed as a mother. My older children had grown up with a depressed, chronically ill, angry mother. My younger two got a mother who was not only angry and in a wheelchair, but one who'd shipped them off to family, abandoning them in relief.

I pondered what life would look like for my family if I weren't there. Chad was young enough he could remarry. A healthy, beautiful woman would step in, be a mother to my children, and give them the home life they deserved. I would miss my children, but they would be happier with a mother who could take care of them. As for me, I'd finally be able to rest. In heaven, I wouldn't be in a wheelchair. In my imagination, I replaced my short, thin hair with long, thick hair that fell in gentle waves around my face. Without a body, my spirit would be free to fly in a place where evil wasn't allowed to enter. I'd been fighting my path of escape from this dark and dreary place. In the space of an hour, I moved from fighting to live to welcoming death. It was the solution I'd been searching for.

I began to pray.

God, if I'm going to die, please give Chad a second lifetime of love and my kids an amazing mother. Thank you for showing me I have nothing to be afraid of.

How long will it take to die? Will I have another attack and be gone, or will I waste away in bed while I watch everyone around me suffer? Please don't make me have to watch.

I'm looking forward to heaven. Life has been so hard. I'm ready to have peace.

God, I did everything you asked. I know I walked away for a while and messed up my life. Thank you for getting me out of that first, abusive marriage. Thank you for giving me a mother to pray over me every day I was gone and who put up with me when I was so horrible.

When I made the choice to follow you again, I never looked back. I did my best to do everything you asked. All I ask is that you help my family. Amber and Gavin already lost their birth mothers, so please keep them from being bitter about losing me too.

Chad is going to have a hard time. Send someone to help the kids while he is grieving. Please send him a wonderful woman quickly. I don't want him to be lonely. I wouldn't mind if she was hot. Chad deserves a good-looking, loving, amazing woman. And make sure she's healthy—someone who can support Chad for the years he's supported me.

I hope my kids aren't too sad on their wedding days, but I will be there, right? They might not see me, but they will feel me, and I'll still get to be there. I'll miss them, but I'll get to see Grandma and Grandpa again. I've missed them.

A peace descended, and I became excited that I would be able to escape this dreary world.

Day by day, the looming grip of death tightened its hold. Chad didn't want to accept what was happening, but I knew it was sure. My paralytic attacks slowed because I was too weak to use my muscles to cause another one. I began wondering if I would go to sleep one night and never wake up.

Mormons believe in special blessings for the healing of the sick. They have consecrated oil to anoint a recipient's head, and it requires at least two men to give these types of blessings.

Chad, along with a fellow church member, had given me one of these blessings earlier and asserted that it wasn't my time to die. I'd thought he was inserting his own wishes into the blessing, so this time, we asked a leader from our church— someone who wasn't as closely involved and less likely to be swayed by what he wanted for me—to be spokesman. Chad wanted me to keep fighting, and I wanted him to accept the inevitable.

We set an appointment and a few days later went to the office of a lay leader over the nine congregations in our area that were collectively called our stake. After the small talk, Chad squeezed a drop of the holy oil onto my head, and they got started. After a few words of comfort, the stake president said, "It is not your time to leave this earth . . . you will be healed in the Lord's time." The words lodged themselves in my heart. God wasn't going to let me die, even after all I had done to prove myself. On the way out, this man looked at me and said, "With all the advances in medicine, there has to be a doctor out there who can help you, even with a disease on the cellular level."

I nodded. I knew I was going to live, but it didn't bring me the peace it did my husband. My task was to fight my way back to health on a long, weary journey with no end in sight. My distaste for the phrase "Endure to the end" heightened.

Chad helped me into the car, and I stared out the window into the darkness of the evening. I wanted peace and rest, but God had refused to give it to me, even as my body crept toward death. I thought of the amazing young people who had left this earth in the prime of their lives, those who were goodness personified. Somewhere I was told God needed them in heaven. Obviously he didn't need me, nor want me, there. He wanted me to suffer under burdens that were too heavy to bear.

7

HOPE

If I had to live, I wasn't going to do it from my bed. My cousin told me about an alternative-care doctor who'd healed her son of severe food allergies. Western medicine had given me a diagnosis and a wheelchair; perhaps Eastern medicine could do better.

In early February, Chad wheeled me into a small office hidden away from the busy streets. A man with a receding hairline and genuine smile walked in. "Hi, I'm Dr. Goulding. Tell me what brings you in today."

I gave Dr. Goulding my history with no expectations that he would know how to help. He explained muscle reactivation through acupressure, NAET allergy treatments, and how those, combined with chiropractic care, would help strengthen my muscles so I could walk again.

We headed to an exam room, where I shifted from my wheelchair onto the chiropractic table. Dr. Goulding poked here and there while asking me to resist as he pulled on my arm, but I had no idea what he was doing.

He looked at me with concern. "Your organs are trying to shut down."

"Yeah." Knowing it wasn't my time to die hadn't shed the hold death had on me.

He tested me for allergens and found food allergies in addition to the environmental allergies I already knew about. Then he started chiropractic adjustments.

"Your atlas is out. That is the top bone of your spine. When it is out of place, it can block the spinal cord, which sends messages from your brain to your muscles. Since we know you have a problem getting those signals to your body, we want to keep the spine aligned so that the channel is as open as possible."

He rolled my head from side to side. "Just relax." One more roll and then he jerked, popping several vertebrae in my neck.

"Roll over onto your stomach."

I rolled over, and he adjusted up and down my back.

"We are going to have to take things very slowly, as you mentioned several times that if you push your body, you crash. I can't do anything about the attacks of paralysis, but I can get you out of the wheelchair and walking again." I missed walking; it would certainly make life easier.

Twice a week, Chad and I drove to Dr. Goulding's office and paid out of pocket since our insurance didn't cover this type of treatment. After each chiropractic adjustment, he'd use acupressure to reactivate my muscles. If I was strong enough, we'd do an allergy treatment.

My sessions with Dr. Goulding required flexibility to push myself and then be able to rest. I thanked God every day for Mom and my sister-in-law Jen, who helped my kids flourish.

Bit by bit, my energy returned and death retreated. I was able to walk to the kitchen by myself, then do a load of dishes. My brain came back online, and I started driving again. I read books and lived in a bubble of peace. Alternative medicine had given me back my life.

With my increased health, Dad became eager for Gavin to move home so he could travel again. Dr. Goulding warned me I wasn't strong enough, but I felt guilty for imposing on them. I told Mom to bring Gavin home but arranged for Jen to keep Amber until the end of the school year, which I hoped would help me ease into having all my kids home without my health crashing.

It didn't take long for my health to decline, but we survived until Amber moved home a few months later. Amber and Gavin weren't oil and water; they were fire and gasoline. The stress taxed my already weakened system, and I returned to long days in bed as the summer stretched on. By the time school started up again, I was back in the wheelchair and continued to decline. I was far better off than before I started alternative care, but I couldn't return due to the financial strain.

A year had passed since my first attack, and it was time for a follow-up appointment with my neuromuscular specialist, Dr. Smith. After a long fight with the insurance, Mom paid for a genetic test so I could enter a clinical trial that would give me better care.

At the clinic, two medical students ran me through the standard strength and reflex tests.

"Are there any new symptoms?" the shorter of the two men said.

"I have these jerks at night, and they've gotten worse. I didn't bring them up before because I've been having them for at least twenty years. I used to get three every night, like clockwork, but lately I get ten to fifteen a night over a two-hour time period, and my muscles jerk hard enough to shake the whole bed. I can't sleep, and I've woken my husband with them."

One medical student entered the information into my file as the other one began to test my muscle strength. The test had never been difficult or strenuous before; it was simply a quick measurement. Now, I had to use all my strength for that second or two, and afterward, each muscle was exhausted and aching. It only took a minute, but when they were done, I was short of breath and dizzy. It scared me to know how much strength I'd lost.

When it was time to check my reflexes, everything went normally until he hit my knees and the spasm not only kicked my leg out but jerked my whole leg. It was so unusual he repeated the motion, causing my shoulder on that side to jerk as well.

"That has never happened before," I said.

The students finished entering all the information into the computer and read it back to me to make sure it was accurate.

Chad and I sat and held hands while we waited for Dr. Smith. He finally entered with a huge smile on his face. "Great news. Your genetic tests were negative. You don't have periodic paralysis," he said as he leaned against the exam table across from where I sat.

That couldn't be right. "What about the 30 percent that show negative but still have it?"

"This test was definitive; there were no mutations found. You don't have periodic paralysis."

Shock numbed me. There would be no study to help, no cure to give me a decent quality of life. Why wouldn't God let me die?

"We are going to start back at square one and rule things out, one by one. Looking back over your file, I noticed you never had a muscle biopsy. That will help us determine what muscle disease you have."

I tuned out. I'd been misdiagnosed for a year. I stared at the white tiles on the floor with their little gray specks.

Dr. Smith continued. ". . . well-tolerated test. I'll make a half-inch incision and using a needle remove three cores of muscle about the size of pencil erasers. It will be scheduled on either a Monday or Friday in the morning."

"Okay." Pencil erasers—that was big. Doctors inflicted pain saying it wouldn't hurt or that a procedure was well tolerated. I wondered what the measure of tolerance was—whether a patient screamed or not?

"Have you ever been tested for myasthenia gravis?"

My brain struggled with the change of topic. "I'm pretty sure we ruled that out, but I don't remember a specific test."

Other things came out of his mouth, but my brain was caught in a whirlwind of possibilities of what might be wrong with me. My wheelchair was here to stay, and with that, there was no hope. Either I would live a long time dependent on Chad or I'd slowly deteriorate, unless they found a cause.

"Do you have any questions?" Dr. Smith asked.

"No."

"Okay, then, I'll have Abby come back to schedule your tests." With that, Dr. Smith was gone.

The expensive potassium monitor I'd purchased was now useless. I'd faithfully been taking high doses of potassium. What if that had damaged my kidneys? Or my liver?

Abby set up the appointments for me, even though I didn't want to do them. I had no choice. I needed to fight for my chance to enjoy life. Chad pushed my wheelchair out of the room and down the long, bland hall.

The double doors swished open, and we were outside. What if I had something worse, like multiple sclerosis or cancer? My blood tests would have shown if I had cancer, though, right?

Across the road and into the dark parking garage we went. Without a diagnosis, there was no treatment. No treatment meant no getting better, no control. I heaved myself into the car. Chad put my wheelchair away and started the engine. I turned on the music and turned off my brain.

At home, I saw Calvin first. "I don't have periodic paralysis."

"I knew it! I knew you didn't have it, otherwise you would have gotten better by now. I did all that research, and I knew you didn't have it." He thought it was good news. I looked over at Nicole, who had overheard us. She looked at me with hope in her eyes for the first time in a year.

As the evening wore on, we all absorbed the news. All this time my mother had said this diagnosis didn't feel right. Being misdiagnosed for a year made me angry. When the anger wore off, worry and helplessness took up residence. The unknown swallowed my hope. I needed to know what was wrong with me.

A week later, I returned for the biopsy. When the nurse mentioned I would remain conscious, with only a local anesthetic, my anxiety swelled.

Several people entered the room with my doctor, and I focused on sounding normal and looking at them as little as possible. I lay there in a hospital gown, even though they were planning on taking the muscle cores out of my shin. My shin made no sense, but I said nothing.

"Can I listen to music?" I asked.

"Sure."

"Chad, can you get my phone and headphones out of my purse, please?" Chad brought me the items, and I busied myself with finding some soothing music. I kept it low so I could still hear while at the same time trying to ignore everyone as much as possible. I didn't want to know, I didn't want to be awake, and I didn't want to be here. I was at the mercy of a handful of men, completely helpless to stop what I'd agreed to.

I made it through the painful shots without screaming. I'd had lots of shots, but these hurt more than any of the others. I shut my eyes, trying to pretend I was somewhere else, trying not to act like a baby.

"That's the hardest part," Dr. Smith reassured me as a tear threatened to betray me. I opened my eyes to prevent it falling and blinked away the moisture, hoping no one had noticed. It was just like when I had to get a shot as a kid. Everyone had praised me for being brave and strong, only letting one tear leak from my eye, but inside I'd screamed and hadn't understood why others wanted to hurt me.

The doctors sat and talked while they waited for the medication to take effect, but I wasn't listening.

I felt a knife cut into my shin but didn't know if that was normal or not. Then a loud machine turned on, amping up my anxiety.

"You'll feel a little pressure."

Why lie to me? *Little* is not the word I'd use to describe what I felt. I wanted to kick the doctors and run screaming from the room, but I kept perfectly still, reminding myself I needed to do this so they could find out what was wrong and fix me.

Time slowed as I lay helpless and trapped by doctors with the power to inflict pain for my good. Then the machine stopped.

"I took five cores to make sure we got good samples, and we're all done," Dr. Smith said.

Five! He'd said three. More lies.

He taped me up and left with his group as if nothing out of the ordinary happened. The nurse said, "You can get dressed now" and left as well. I sat up and got my first look at what they had done to me.

There was a red line about an inch long running parallel to my shin bone. He'd said it would only be a half inch. It was probably only a half inch, but it looked huge. Of course, he'd also said three cores and he'd taken five. He'd probably lied about the length too. Clear tape had been placed over the cut, pulling my skin together. He'd kept taping until I had a huge asterisk covering the front of my leg.

"That was fascinating to watch," Chad said.

"How big were the chunks he took out?" How much of my body was missing?

"They were small—like a large needle and about as deep as my pinky nail." Not as big as a pencil eraser; as deep as a pencil eraser. I marginally relaxed while Chad helped me get dressed.

Chad drove me home, where I sat in our recliner for days, exhausted. It took me an entire week to recover, not the two or three days I was promised. Almost a month later, Chad and I returned to Dr. Smith's office for the results.

I braced myself for bad news, but my biopsies returned normal. Dr. Smith explained that though there were abnormalities, it didn't match any known muscle diseases and still fell within the range of normal. The myasthenia gravis test also returned normal.

I hadn't prepared myself for the tests to be negative. The rest of my life stretched out before me. I would spend it in a wheelchair, and no one knew why. Sitting across from the doctor, I sobbed. Any diagnosis was better than no diagnosis.

"Basically, I don't know why you are in that wheelchair. Unfortunately, that happens more often than we like." It was the only explanation Dr. Smith could give me, and it offered no comfort.

"We still have the electromyography, or EMG, scheduled. I don't expect it to uncover anything, but it will definitely rule out several muscle disorders."

Several weeks later, I returned for the painful test, where a needle was inserted into my muscle and moved around while mild jolts of electricity were run through the tissue.

I hated every second of the torture. My body began jerking and wouldn't stop. Eventually, they switched to my other arm.

I sat there helplessly, hooked up to machines with needles digging around inside me, when my body suddenly took over. The arm no longer attached to the machines began to wave and jerk, completely out control. I was a marionette under the power of some unseen force pulling my strings, but it got me out of the rest of the test.

The pain was wasted when this test returned normal as well. I had healthy muscles that weren't getting the signals from my brain. The remaining option was to see a psychiatrist. Dr. Smith knew a specialist who treated brain injuries. He could rewire my brain to communicate with my muscles again.

A psychiatrist. Dr. Smith must have concluded I was crazy too. After my tests were negative when I was twenty-six, the neurologist wanted me to see a therapist for anxiety, thinking that was what was causing my periodic paralysis. If it was in my head, I could control it. But I had no control. I wanted someone to give me medicine to fix my body or I wanted God to let me die.

I let Dr. Smith give me the information for the referral, but I wasn't going to call the doctor. My mental state crumbled to dust. God hadn't healed me, Eastern medicine could only go so far, and Western had medicine turned out to be nothing but expensive torture. My fight died.

8
HEALING

I woke up every morning whether I wanted to or not. There was no escape, so I decided to keep working at the only option I had left—God. Three times God had promised to heal me, in his own time. Either it wasn't time or I lacked faith. I spent hours studying and praying, focusing on miracles of healing.

I didn't understand how Jesus healed people immediately. It made no sense. I lived in my body. I knew how much time and energy each piece of healing took.

I knew God had created me and that he knew more about my body than a doctor could learn in a lifetime. I knew he perfectly understood science, that he held the power of the universe, and that his word was perfect. Yet knowing this didn't translate into belief. Still, I continued to study and think about miracles.

I read a book called *Visions of Glory*, as told to John Pontius, which relates the near-death experiences and visions of someone named only as Spencer. I always read such books with caution, gathering the bits that ring true to me and allowing the rest to fall away like reading fiction. During one of his near-death experiences, he talked about walking through walls and furniture. He knew everything about the desk, from the life of the three trees it was made of to the pleasure a living thing had in being created into a desk to be of use to man. The wood had no will of its own but a tiny bit of intelligence. All living things had a greater or lesser degree of intelligence, with human beings at the pinnacle of God's creations.

It never made sense to me how an individual stem cell knew what type of cell it should become. If DNA was the blueprint, and a developing fetus had no brain, how did the first cells know what to do? I'd concluded that God guided the process. There was no other explanation. If there was enough intelligence put into a tree to become a living thing to serve man and glorify God, it was possible that each cell in my body had a bit of intelligence as well. Research showed that trauma changed DNA, meaning DNA was a blueprint that could be updated.

When the lumberjack chopped down the tree, it ceased to live but still contained intelligence. I was not only alive but the pinnacle of God's creations. God created me and my body. He knew how to communicate with whatever intelligence was in each of my cells. It was God's will that I be healed, but I believed he had given me moral agency to make choices for myself and would not force his will on me.

Earlier in the year, there was no medical reason for my body to move toward death. I remembered my longing to die, my disappointment when I was told God wanted me to live. What if I chose death and it was enough to alter the functioning of my body? If I chose life, could God whisper to every cell in my body to fix what was wrong?

It happened in a fraction of a second: one moment I didn't understand, and the next I did. I understood how Christ could instantly change every cell in my body. A warm feeling enveloped me. There was intelligence in my cells. The atonement of Christ was available not only for repentance but also for the healing of mind and body. Trauma might have changed my DNA, but God created my body and knew how to speak to it. Christ was the same now as he was in times of old when he healed through his power those who were sick. If there is some form of intelligence, even very small, like a simple computer code, God could ask a mountain to move and it would obey. With my permission, he could speak to my body, even to every cell, and ask them to change, using the power he held, and it could happen instantly. I treasured this new understanding and waited patiently for healing.

Physically, I had come full circle. I spent most of my days in bed, but my brain function stayed high. The weakness felt different, but I couldn't pinpoint why.

One crisp Saturday morning, I woke to a strange sensation. Every cell in my body was awake and functioning. The sluggishness was gone.

I remained cautious, having ridden the roller coaster of energy up and down for years and accepted each day as a gift in case my healing was only temporary. I enjoyed Thanksgiving, shopped for Christmas, and celebrated the birth of Christ with my family.

I counted back to the last attack and realized I'd gone three months without an attack, then four. It took that long for me to accept that I had been healed by God.

My muscles didn't gain strength immediately, but they became stronger each day. After being in a wheelchair for a year, Mom told me to expect it to take a year to recover. I tried to be patient, but there were many days I pushed my weakened body beyond what it was ready to handle.

I met with Dr. Smith, who declared I was experiencing a spontaneous remission. Everything within me rejected the idea that this was a period of remission similar to my past. I knew my body had been reborn.

I celebrated every milestone: the first day I was able to lift my wheelchair out of the car by myself, the day I began making dinner for my family again, my first trip to the basement in over a year.

As soon as I was strong enough, I began saying yes to everything that came my way. I wanted to make up for all I'd missed, from helping out at the school to signing up to help others in need. That pace caused mental and physical exhaustion to the point sleep no longer erased it.

Anger, betrayal, and pain stole my newfound health. The attacks of paralysis were gone, but the fatigue had returned, and I knew it was because of stress and poor management of my mental health.

I slowed down and started working on the exercises in a book my alternative care doctor had recommended, *The Emotion Code*, by Dr. Bradley Nelson. In the past, I'd refused to consider anything off the traditional medical path, but I was more open now.

I learned about the connection between emotions and the body and how the body is full of energy and currents. If there is a disruption in the energy, the body doesn't function properly. Many traumatic memories are stored throughout the body and cause disruptions of energy. Dr. Nelson called them trapped emotions.

Chad read questions aloud from the book while I swayed forward for a yes and backward for a no. It was an odd sensation because the stronger the answer, the more I swayed.

We narrowed the trapped emotion to one square in the grid, and Chad asked, "Is the trapped emotion crying?"

I slowly nudged backward.

"Is the trapped emotion discouragement?"

Same response.

"Is the trapped emotion rejection?"

A more hesitant sway backward. Did we do something wrong?

"Is the trapped emotion sadness?"

I immediately swayed forward. Through a series of questions, we identified what the emotion stemmed from, and a memory popped into my head.

It was right before my fortieth birthday, mere months earlier. It was highly significant day for me, and I wanted to celebrate with a huge party. No one seemed to like turning forty, but it was a milestone to me.

I'd dreamed and looked forward to that day ever since I'd turned thirty, but I never imagined I'd be in a wheelchair. I'd mourned the loss of my dreams weeks beforehand.

It ended up being a great day because Chad had picked as many items off my bucket list as he could and fulfilled them.

Chad picked up the golden medical grade magnet from its box. I could have purchased any strong magnet, but I loved the shape and look of this magnet made for easy holding to ease chronic pain. He began running the magnet down my spine.

It felt good, but there was nothing spectacular about it. As I thought about all this, I remembered my mother being upset at turning forty. She hadn't wanted to celebrate it, and there was nothing I could do to lighten her mood. I saw the meager offering I'd labored over—a half apron trimmed in lace with a pocket that had all the raw edges showing. Judging from the house I remember being in, I was ten years old. I needed to celebrate my fortieth birthday because my mom hadn't been able to celebrate hers.

I'd been skeptical of the whole process, but it worked. Long-forgotten memories were pulled to the surface, processed, and released with the help of the strong magnet. Sometimes it triggered nightmares as my brain continued to process things I'd shoved down for years.

Looking closely at my life, I realized that I wasn't good with relationships. I began opening myself up to the truth of who I was and seeing things that didn't make sense.

I had forgiven Carson for our abusive relationship but wasn't able to let go of judgmental comments that had hurt me. I also began to see the ways I'd contributed to our disastrous marriage. We were two emotionally crippled people trying to force the other to love them by tearing them down. I was equally at fault, and I hated myself for it. I'd spent years blaming him when I'd contributed to our toxic relationship just as much.

I'd alternately pulled acquaintances too close, desperate for connection, and pushed family members away, unable to communicate my needs and distress. I'd resented everyone who looked at me oddly, ignored me, or didn't show the type of caring I wanted from them.

I tapped into deep wells of pain, discovered errors in my thinking, and realized that I was a mess inside. I wondered how these problems affected my health.

I'd seen my current therapist, Susan off and on for several years. She was like a favorite grandma, the fun one with a soft smile and big squishy hug that created the safest place on earth. She never gave a hug without asking and had no problem when I said no. She was the best therapist I'd ever had.

Over the months, Susan and I tackled my emotional issues. I learned about cognitive-behavior therapy to shape the negative self-talk I barraged myself with, discovered what boundaries were, and practiced implementing them in my life. With new social skills, I began taking charge of my life.

I learned that forgiveness meant letting go of any judgments, pain, bitterness, and thoughts of revenge. I didn't have to condone what someone did, understand why they did it, or make sure they knew how much they had hurt me.

The thing that prevented me from forgiving was not that God wasn't willing to take those feelings away but that I was holding on to them. One day I let go, and God took it. I snatched it back before letting God take it again.

One by one, I forgave the people who hurt me. My body became stronger, and I was able to use my energy for something better than holding grudges.

At home, I kept working on the emotion code until I was ready to tackle what Dr. Nelson called the "heart wall." I'd always known I kept a huge wall between myself and others. It was time to dismantle it enough to let others in.

I began by using visualization to discover what my heart wall looked like. In our imaginations we can fly, be superheroes, or hold the entire world on the tip of our finger. A heart wall can be represented by anything. It can be soft, hard, stone, steel, thick, or thin.

My heart wall looked like a fortress deep in a dark, thorny wood. I was safe inside the fortress, snuggled in a cozy space of soft fur, which I stroked like a child does her special blankie.

The walls of my fortress were thick and secure, with no entrances or windows. Surrounding the fortress was a huge stone wall with no gate. Partially encased in this wall were dozens of snarling wolves ready to devour anyone who came near. There was only a narrow space before thick brambles began, tangled with long, sharp thorns on the edge of the dark, foreboding forest. The entire area was covered in a damp, gray fog.

No wonder people stayed away. I wanted to remove the wall, let my energy flow, and let sunshine into my heart. As soon as I thought about it, the love I had for my heart wall surged forward. I looked closer at the little girl inside that fortress. In her little nook, she was safe, comfortable, and loved. I couldn't take that safety away from her.

My heart wall stayed up, but I continued to work on identifying and healing other parts of my life. As I worked through my issues, a wolf would be freed and run off into the forest, taking my anger and hate with it.

One lazy afternoon, I lay next to Chad, letting my mind wander toward sleep. Inside, I felt as if something were smothering me and I couldn't breathe. I touched my stomach, reassured that air flowed in and out, but the sensation refused to leave.

I touched the tight confines of my heart wall. It was suffocating my heart. The fortress I loved no longer protected me; it was killing me.

The little girl inside gasped for air as the walls narrowed in on her. She pushed against the soft, fuzzy walls, desperate to break out. I channeled strength to her, and she began to grow like Alice in Wonderland. As she grew, the space became smaller, pushing her arms close to her body, hunching her over in the tiny womb of my own making.

"Run away!" she yelled to the wolves. The couple dozen that remained jumped free and ran as a pack into the wilderness.

The girl pushed with her back against the constraint while spreading her arms wide. The fur split apart, freeing her, and she took a deep breath of fresh, spring air.

She looked down at the pieces of fur at her feet and at the bricks that no longer formed a wall, and noticed she was high above the forest and brambles, in the light of the sky and clouds.

I opened my eyes. A new sense of vulnerability left me feeling naked and exposed. Air and energy flowed through my body in a different way.

Everything around me looked and felt different. It was like seeing color for the first time. The flowers were brighter, I heard birdsong outside my window, and I appreciated my husband more.

Yet with this expansion of awareness and love came the ability to be hurt more deeply, and I retreated from unsafe people until my discomfort faded. It was scary to be myself and not pretend or hide, but the trade-off was increased joy and aliveness.

My energy increased as I allowed myself to feel the pain and then for the hurt to be washed away, and I used my wheelchair less and less. This process wasn't quick or easy. It took time for my muscles to rebuild themselves, time to learn forgiveness, and time to learn how to live.

Chad and I needed space to recover from the stress of my illness, so we drove from Utah to Oregon through the desert. Once we neared the Columbia River, everything turned green. We stayed at a bed-and-breakfast that looked out on the river and enjoyed the crisp air, which was a welcome break from the heat of a Utah summer.

We drove to the Multnomah Falls and gazed from afar at the beauty. I wanted to walk up to get a closer look, but I wasn't strong enough. In that moment, I decided to get my strength back. I wanted to experience the world on my own two feet. My life was no longer an unwelcome burden forced on me by God but a gift I had accepted.

We skirted past Portland, forgoing the sights in the city in favor of the coast. When we arrived at our next bed-and-breakfast, we parked and headed straight for the beach, less than a block away. An older couple with their grandchildren, a woman jogging the shoreline, and a couple romping with their dog were the only people within a mile of us.

I wanted to romp with the dog, jog with the woman, and play with the grandchildren. For most, the simple act of walking on the beach was something taken for granted, but for me it was a miracle.

I took off my shoes and squished my toes into the warm sand. I inhaled the cool breeze blowing inland. Healing energy seemed to wash in with every wave, allowing me to take a short walk with Chad. We sauntered just out of reach of the waves in a bubble of contentment. We walked farther than I thought I'd be able to go, but I stopped worrying about my body crashing later. I lived only in that exquisite moment.

I thought about the man walking next to me. He'd stood by me through two years of illness, showing rare commitment in our fast-paced, divorce-riddled world.

"I love you," I said.

"I love you too." He squeezed my hand.

We wandered up to where the sun had warmed the sand and sat down to watch the ocean. "I'm glad we skipped Portland to get here early."

"Me too," Chad replied.

"It's so relaxing."

"Mm-hmmm." I glanced over to see his head tilted back, his eyes closed.

I leaned back on the sand, and he followed suit. The sand warmed me from beneath while the breeze kept me cool. The waves crashed, blocking everything else out, and my stress floated away.

I remembered old books where doctors prescribed a change of location and a trip to the cool beaches for healing. I'd never understood it until that moment, soaking up the vitality of the ocean.

Eventually, we got up and headed to the bed-and-breakfast, where we learned that the name, Pana-Sea-Ah Bed and Breakfast, was a spin on panacea, a remedy for all ills, physical and mental.

Our stay was magical, restorative to both body and soul. I didn't want to leave after only one night and vowed to return. We continued down the coast with strength in my body I marveled at. Taking care of my emotional well-being was just as important as exercise or eating nourishing food. In the absence of the stress of daily living, my energy abounded.

I took that lesson home with me and took self-care more seriously. I rarely used my wheelchair when I got home, and soon it had sat in the garage for a month. On a beautiful fall day, I took my wheelchair apart and stored it in the attic under a sheet, where it stayed.

I forgave God for making me fight my way back to health rather than escape through death. He had seen what I could not, that my life had the possibility of richness and beauty.

My gratitude for a working body stayed with me. Having had a taste of living gave me a thirst for more. Witnessing the affect my emotional state had on my physical health made me ponder why I'd been both chronically ill and chronically depressed for so many years of my life. The depression hit when my parents moved to Salt Lake City shortly after my fifteenth birthday and rarely lifted until I began taking antidepressants in my mid-thirties.

The chronic illness started when I married Carson and worsened for years before I experienced my first short burst of health. I didn't want this newfound energy to be another short burst. I felt like a ticking time bomb and wondered how much living I could squeeze into whatever time I had. At night fears of my paralysis returning turned dreams into nightmares.

The months in bed with only my mind for company confirmed that something else lurked deep within my psyche. Mom often said I had a horrible childhood. I didn't pay much attention because her comments were usually combined with what a bad mother she'd been or how poor we were. It made me uncomfortable to hear her talk like that. In those lonely hours of sickness, I had reconnected with my body and sensed a locked room of darkness inside me that I'd often mentioned in my journals when

I was a teen and early adult. Whatever had created that dark space within my soul must have happened in my childhood.

During the day I kept busy, but in the quiet times when sleep refused to come, that room haunted me. To move forward and truly learn how to live, I needed to revisit my past. I began digging into the portion of my childhood that never did live in peace. Only darkness.

9

DIGGING

The need to understand my life gnawed at me. Mom said it was the work of the forties. Maybe now the puzzle pieces would finally combine to reveal their hidden picture.

I began with my ex-husband, Carson. I read through my journals, shocked to see a different person emerging through the pages. The emotional abuse he inflicted on me was clear; why I allowed it was not.

I thought I could walk away from the past when I left Carson. I met Chad and built a new life. It was ten years into my marriage before I understood that in closing the door on what happened, I never allowed myself to heal.

Chad and I had moved to Wisconsin for a job around the time I gave up on any medical solutions to my paralysis. My chronic depression became debilitating, and I finally sought out a therapist. It was my first brush with a therapy called EMDR, or eye movement desensitization and reprocessing, to help me heal from the abuse of my first marriage.

#memory

I sat in the gray parking lot looking at the gray building, where even the windows reflected the gray sky that typified Wisconsin for me. I didn't want to go inside.

But I had no choice, so I got up and went in. The lobby was filled with dull colors and grim faces snuggled in dark coats and faded blue jeans against mustard seats. I wrote my name on a sign-in sheet and sat down in my hot-pink ski jacket. My heart thumped as if I were caught in the crosshairs of a gun, waiting for the squeeze of a trigger.

My middle-aged blonde therapist retrieved me, and I followed her through the maze of hallways to her door. I sat in the stiff chair opposite the sofa while she sat behind her desk.

"Are you ready to start?"

"Sure." My eyes darted to her before staring out the window at the parking lot.

"We are helping those traumatic experiences that got trapped in the brain get processed so they can be released." She walked around the desk and put a chair in the middle of the room, facing where I sat. "Sit right here."

I moved to the other chair while she sat in the spot I had vacated. My face flushed at occupying her seat.

"You don't need to tell me anything that is happening, but every so often I'm going to ask you a question to make sure you're okay. If you want to share, you are welcome to do so. I'll start by moving my two fingers back and forth in front of your eyes, and you just need to follow. I might switch to tapping on your leg or your arm to keep the rhythm going when my hand gets tired."

I nodded.

"Just remember that you aren't in the situation. Most people say it's like they are watching a movie. But you are here, and you are safe. If we need to stop, raise your hand. Are you ready?"

My mouth said yes while my heart screamed no.

She started moving her fingers back and forth, and I traced them with my eyes.

"Start with any memory while you follow my fingers with your eyes."

Her fingers faded into the background. For a moment nothing happened, then I saw Carson tying my arms to the bed to act out a rape.

The terry robe sash bound my hands above my head to the headboard. I tugged in discomfort, but they were secure.

I wanted him off me, to stop this charade.

My pent-up anger overflowed. "No!" I cried. My hollow words merely played into his fantasy.

"No . . ." I shook my head.

"No." I struggled against his body, but it merely excited him, adding heat to his fire.

"No." Fear and pain reared up, drowning out all rational thought.

"No!" I yelled as the game he played out on my body became real.

He rarely finished quickly, savoring his control, his fantasy my nightmare.

It's only a movie. My mind pulled back. I sat in a dark theater while the images kept moving on the screen.

Before I could raise my hand to stop, I noticed a man sitting in the dark movie theater with me. I turned and saw Jesus. He wasn't going to make me go through this alone.

"I will be right here with you the whole time." His words emanated from him, interwoven with strength and love.

He exuded strength, and I leaned into it. He embraced me with a compassion and understanding that allowed me to continue.

"You need to do this important work," he said. "You need to walk through this dark place, but it will end, and you will step into the light without these burdens you carry."

Scenes continued playing out in front of me, worse than I remembered them being, but the steady presence of Jesus never left me.

I finally saw the depth of the abuse. I marveled that I had escaped and built a better life for myself. Whenever I started to resist, added strength radiated from my Savior.

Lost in this world of darkness, I wasn't aware of the passage of time. The scenes played out until my therapist pulled me back into the fluorescent light of the dreary office. The subtle presence of Jesus remained.

"We are out of time for today. How are you feeling?"

I lied. "I'm fine."

"Just because we stop doesn't mean the brain stops processing." She held out a card, and I took it. "All of my numbers are on there. You can call me day or night. It can be frightening when memories return." She touched my arm and looked into my eyes. "You can sit in the waiting room as long as you need to."

"I have to go pick up my daughter from the babysitter."

"Is there anyone who can watch her? This first little bit is the hardest part."

"No. But I'll be fine." I needed to return to the safety of my house.

I hustled to my car, got in, and hesitated before turning the key in the ignition. I shoved down the images from the session.

In a daze, I picked up Nicole, grateful I had a couple of hours before Ethan and Calvin arrived home on the bus. I distracted myself as much as possible, barely talking. I was in shock.

A couple of days later, as I drifted off to sleep in my cozy bed, I felt a hand grab my neck, pushing against my windpipe. My eyes flew open, but no one was there, and yet the imprint of the hand tingled against my throat. I tried to rationalize the sensation away, but the phantom hand refused to let go.

My cheeks became wet as my emotions bubbled to the surface, then exploded. In a panic, I shook my husband awake.

"I remember a hand on my neck strangling me, but it never happened." I wrapped my fingers around my throat, placing each finger where the pressure lingered. "It was like this. I was trapped, and I didn't like it, but that never happened. She said I would remember things I'd forgotten, but how can I remember something that never happened?"

"Shh, it's okay," Chad said, wrapping his arms around me and snuggling me close. "I'm here, and you're safe."

With my head against his chest, I listened to his heartbeat, secure in his arms.

I gasped. "I remember. It did happen."

I clutched Chad's arm. "Carson did that to me. He wasn't trying to strangle me; he was cutting off the blood to my brain. He heard that it would give us an extra high while having sex. I hated it. Every time his body pushed against me, the pressure of his hand on my neck increased. I wanted him to stop and leave me alone."

I cried out into the darkness, "Why did he do that to me?"

89

"I'm sorry, honey. It's okay. You're safe now."

Tears caused my nose to run, and I needed a tissue, but I didn't want to leave the comfort of the only safety I knew. "He wanted me to do it to him, and he got upset at me because I never pushed hard enough. I tried, but I didn't want to hurt him. Yet he had no problem hurting me. Why did I marry him? I knew it was a bad decision, but I did it anyway. I can't do this. I want to stop. I don't want to remember anything else."

"I know. It's okay."

I didn't need words from Chad; I only needed his strong arms to always be there, holding me. Here was someone who loved me enough to hold all my broken pieces together until they mended. He had always been there for me.

He held me until my tears dried and the shuddering of my body ceased. As I calmed, the undeniable presence of God comforted me, and the last of my terror drained away. God encircled me about in a bubble of safety and peace.

Finally, I drifted off.

I plowed through my memories with EMDR, and though it was a brutal process, after three months I'd let go of the baggage I'd been lugging around for ten years.

While I remembered the abuse the EMDR had brought up, I didn't remember anything else. I had basic facts I recited to others but no understanding of what had happened to create such a toxic situation. The logical conclusion was that whatever issues still plagued me must have come from that relationship.

Now I sat in different bland lobby, though a more pleasing mix of maroon and blue-gray while I waited for Susan.

When she appeared, I followed her to her cozy office.

"How are you, Dawn?" she asked.

"Good."

We chatted for a few minutes, and then I got down to business.

"I can recite the basics of what happened with my first husband, Carson, but I don't remember most of it."

"Why do you want to remember it?"

"That relationship messed me up, but I don't know how to fix it because I can't remember. Isn't it weird that I've blocked it out so completely?"

"Have you ever heard of nondominant-hand drawing?"

"No."

Susan opened up her filing drawer and pulled out a small binder. Inside were colored-pencil drawings.

"Whatever hand you normally write with is your dominant hand. That hand represents your adult self. When you draw or write with your nondominant hand, that represents your inner child."

She flipped through a few of the pages she kept in her office to demonstrate. There was a detailed picture of her childhood self, another picture showing where her pain was located, and a dark and angry scrawl depicting the pain she held inside.

"You can ask yourself a question and respond with your nondominant hand," Susan said.

It looked a little crazy to me, but if it would help me uncover my memories and heal, I was willing to give it a try.

Susan and I went on to discuss other difficulties in my life until my appointment ended.

That night, I sat cross-legged on my bed, an array of colored pencils and a few sheets of clean white paper spread out next to me. I didn't know where to start. I began with what Susan suggested, to find out who I was.

I wrote, "Who are you?" with my right hand in pen.

I am Dawn. I love my name. It's pretty. Especially the D. I love to write D, I responded with a blue colored pencil held in my left hand.

"What are you afraid of?"

Carson. He's a bad man. Chad is good and nice, like a big, soft teddy bear, but if Carson came, he'd bite his head off for me. I like Chad a lot.

"How do you know Carson?"

I married him. He was bad and lied. He was mean. God saved me from the bad man.

"How did God save you from the bad man?"

He gave me a family to love me and take care of me, and he told me to leave.

"What was the worst thing the bad man did?"

He tied me up and pretended to rape me. I didn't like it. He treated me like I was stupid. He was mean even when he pretended to be nice. He made me pretend to be bad, but I only wanted to be happy and nice.

I felt schizophrenic, so I switched to drawing a picture of myself. I chose red and began to draw a dress. Next came the arms, legs, and a face with yellow hair and blue eyes. At the bottom I wrote, "I am 6. I am happy. My dress is red with white polka dots. I am cute."

Next, I drew myself as a sad teenager, and then on my wedding day, sad and trapped. Then came Carson as a stick figure stomping and jumping on my figure on the floor while I had a speech bubble that said, "Help!"

He had two speech bubbles, one with an evil laugh and the other saying, "You are bad, bad girl. You suck. You worthless. I better. You my slave forever!"

I sat and stared at the pictures. How had I come to that place? What had transformed me from a happy little girl to a helpless, sullen teenager who'd decided to marry someone who controlled me even before we married? I was terrified the same thing would happen to my own sweet kids. I'd heard writing was therapeutic. Perhaps I needed to write out my experiences with Carson.

I asked my inner child if she wanted to write about the bad man. My other hand responded with a large *YES*.

"Why?" I asked.

I want everyone to be happy in the Son. Jesus is better than the sun. People will be happy and not listen to bad men lie.

"How can I write about the bad man if I don't remember him?"

My inner child seemed to ponder this for a moment. *You can dream. God can send you a dream of the bad man, and then you write it.*

"God will send me a dream?"

If you ask. You have to ask for help, duh. Then he help you. He a good daddy. I want to draw. It's more fun.

My inner child drew a rainbow.

Pretty rainbow. It comes after the rain, see? No rain. No rainbows. I like rainbows.

I gathered up the colored pencils and put everything away.

For months I used the nondominant-hand technique to draw out scenes from my first marriage, encouraging the memories to the surface. My inner child was matter-of-fact with the truth. She was also creative, using whatever tools her imagination gave her to convey the feelings I had buried deep inside.

I learned that my relationship had been much worse than I thought as I contemplated the cumulative damage of our destructive daily interactions. A fresh batch of anger gave way to shame for my part in it and then settled into deep sadness at the result of two people so broken they could do nothing but cut each other down when they tried to get close.

While some abusers hurt their victims and then made it up to them, Carson buttered me up, pressured me until I gave him what he wanted, and then abused me. One day he took me out to a nice dinner we couldn't afford to show me how much he loved me and then had a pornographic movie he'd rented waiting in the bedroom. I hated every bit of the porn he subjected me to over the year a half we were married.

As I continued my journey, I understood how destructive the pornography was to our relationship and how it fed the abuse, creating the need for a bigger and bigger fix. I was his drug of choice.

As a naïve nineteen-year-old, I was shocked at the sudden abusive turn in our relationship, and yet, in hindsight, there were numerous red flags I'd refused to see. He proposed a week after our first date and monopolized my time. My family didn't like him and didn't want me to get married, but I dug in my heels, more determined than ever to marry and escape their control.

It deeply disturbed me that I'd allowed him to push and manipulate me into sex. I never protested, not even after that hated first time. I wasn't happy, but I kept moving toward the wedding, sure that once we were married, everything would be fine. God made sure I knew on my wedding day that it was a mistake, but I ignored the warning.

#memory

I don't want to get married.

The words swirled in my head and gained steam while I sat on my bed, waiting for the ceremony to start. I stared at my hands folded gently in my lap, sure they belonged to someone else. They wrung restlessly while my legs shook. Inside, lions gnawed at my stomach, and natives drummed on my heart.

My brain fought my visceral reactions. *It's just cold feet.*

Plunging temperatures forced us to move everything we'd set up in our backyard into the house before the late-morning ceremony. My best friend, Dave, came over, and we got it finished in plenty of time, with lots of teasing and laughter. The contrast between the fun with Mom and Dave and my dread at marrying Carson hit me.

I'd once seen someone on television standing on a pier get clobbered with a wave that came out of nowhere. An icy dread soaked me as completely as the dripping man I'd seen after the wave receded.

I wanted to lock myself in my room until everyone disappeared.

No. *You're a grown-up. Start acting like it.*

Marriage was the only way to hide my sins. The murmur of the wedding guests reminded me that I'd set the stage. The star of the show couldn't disappear. A quiet knock sounded on the door.

"Dawn?" Mom poked her head into my bedroom, her hand gripping the doorjamb. "It's time. Are you ready?"

"Yes." I stood up, my body knowing what was expected even if my mind felt out of sync. I was being pulled in two different directions.

I left the sanctuary of my bedroom and met Carson at the end of the hall. I handed him the bouquet I'd put together the night before. A new acquaintance and my maid-of-honor, Amanda, and I had sat on her porch the night before, putting together the grocery-store flowers in the frigid temperatures so they wouldn't wilt.

I adjusted the veil to fall over my face. As I took the bouquet back, I realized the ivory roses and deep-purple iris looked lovely after all.

Our fingers brushed each other briefly. "I'm the luckiest man alive," Carson said. "I love you."

"I love you too."

Carson peeked around the corner of the hall and signaled for my mother to push play on the stereo. The first notes of "Canon in D" floated across the living room, and our thirty guests rose.

I stepped out. My rented mermaid-style dress hugged my slim body in front of a cloud of organza ruffles that fell from my waist and trailed several feet behind me.

We headed up the short, narrow aisle. The only way to fit all the chairs in the small living room was to go in at an angle and then straighten out toward the front.

A crooked aisle for a crooked bride.

I knew my guests could see right through me to the scarlet letter I wore inside. I didn't deserve to wear white, and neither did Carson. Not brave enough to be the runaway bride, I made it through the jury and to the judge, who waited to sentence me to life without parole. He spoke, but his string of words tangled before I could make sense of them. I'd never been to a wedding before. My older brothers were married in a Mormon temple; no children allowed.

When the ring was placed on my finger, it felt like a tourniquet, not a symbol of endless love.

I knew that morning I didn't want to marry Carson, but I did it anyway. I told myself it was about disappointing the guests, wasting my parents' money, and needing to grow up. I thought the only way to make things right was to marry the man who had taken my virginity, but two wrongs didn't make a right.

I'd spent the last twenty years blaming teenage stupidity, but I was old enough now to know that wasn't the whole story. There had to be a reason I'd allowed that type of relationship and had given in to his demands. I was a messed up teenager long before I met Carson. I tried to use him to fix myself but broke further. I felt I needed to delve into my childhood to understand why.

For weeks I drew stick figures of myself as a child, each new set more disturbing. They had no hands or feet, then no faces. Sometimes other people on the page were huge, while I was tiny and in the bottom corner.

I was insignificant in my family and tiny next to mean teachers who loomed over me and demanded I do what they wanted. That child wasn't allowed to ask questions or protest, only told to be quiet.

I discovered a deep well of sadness and pain that radiated from a tiny dot on the map of my childhood. Hillview. My family and I were outcasts, poor and isolated. I fought to be accepted in the popular crowd during my middle school years there but ended up being rejected while losing my few true friends in the process. All kids went through that type of upheaval in middle school; it was part of growing up. Of course, most kids didn't sleep in a shed or have the Scouts shove cake into the gas tank of the family car. I needed to remember in order to lay such childish concerns to rest.

I pulled out my paper and colored pencils.

First I drew a stick figure in black. I got out a blue pencil and drew water rising to my mouth, about to drown me.

I returned to the black and scribbled angry clouds above my head, with rain pouring down. A huge, scary mouth and two angry slits for eyes appeared next to me on the page. Then a huge spider with fangs. From the fangs, I drew blood dripping down and falling into a puddle of red.

I wrote in childlike letters underneath, "Go away. Hide. Run. Bad, Bad, Bad."

I labeled the picture, "My childhood."

I took my nondominant-hand drawings to my therapy sessions each week, adding them to a binder that was quickly filling up. Some made sense, but others didn't. After having learned the previous week that the lack of hands and feet represented my helplessness, I needed more information. What was it that had caused me to feel so helpless?

I asked my therapist, "Why don't I have a face in my pictures?"

She smiled cryptically and said, "I noticed that. Why do you think you don't have a face?"

"I don't know."

"Maybe you should ask your inner child that."

That night I wrote, "Why don't you have a face in your pictures?"

I drew two circle dots with a trail of tears going down the page and into a puddle at the bottom. At the top I wrote, "I nobody." In the bottom corner I wrote, "Just go away. I sad."

A few days later, I tried again.

"Why did you draw yourself without a face?"

I drew a blue stick figure with arms covering her face.

I wrote three sentences: "See no evil. Hear no evil. Speak no evil."

My nondominant hand continued because I didn't understand, "See no evil. Only good inside, then happy if blind, deaf, and dumb."

"What do you see and hear and say if you open your eyes, ears, and mouth?" I asked on the next page.

"NO," my other hand wrote in huge letters across the page. "Not going to!"

Until I shed light on the darkness, I would never understand the poor choices I'd made or where the sadness had come from.

10

DISCOVERY

It was on a warm Saturday morning that I resolved to discover the truth. I locked myself away from the kids and sat down on my bed.

I drew myself at a door with a big smile. On the other side of the door was a man who towered over me. He had mean eyes.

"Come in, little girl," he said.

On a new sheet of paper, I drew myself sitting in a chair with no arms or hands. The huge man now held a bag of candy and sported a line to represent his arousal. "Candy?" he asked.

I began another page, trying to force myself not to draw what began taking shape, an aroused man as tall as the page, while I was no bigger than an inch, with only a circle for a head, a stick for a body, and two legs. "Know what this is?" he asked me, referring to the line symbolizing his arousal. In tiny letters above my head, I wrote, "No."

I continued, though each page got worse.

"Wanna touch?" he asked.

"No," I responded, then, "Okay."

Harmless ink was shaped into sickening images until they morphed into words that appeared across the blank space. *Growed-up man. Do what growed-ups say. Saw at church.*

My nondominant hand wrote too slowly for the surfacing memories, so I switched to my other hand and wrote everything I remembered.

I stopped and dropped my pen, staring at nothing. Denial crept forward, but the serpent of truth struck it down. I flipped through the twenty-three pages that had poured out of me. They stared back, evidence that I had been groomed and molested as a child. Someone had found out, blamed me for it, and then threatened me if I ever told anyone.

Flashes of odd behavior paraded past, my sudden change of personality, my shutting my family out, and my being suicidal for five years. My being molested explained why I had gone from happy child to sullen teen.

I began rocking back and forth.

Reality faded along with the crisp outlines of my walls and dresser. The air no longer felt light, it was thick and heavy like water. Pressure weighed me down as I struggled to hear, move, and see clearly. It reminded me of being at the bottom of the swimming pool as a child.

On one side of me, I gripped the shield of denial, on the other the gun of truth. No matter how often I whispered my denials, truth stood firm. The shield dropped, shattering into a thousand shards of deadly glass. *I can't stay here. I need to run away.*

I was a wife and mother trapped in the mind of the little girl I had drawn. All I knew was that I needed to run away from the monster. My legs began moving, my body given no choice but to follow. I opened my bedroom door, walked down the hall, and stood in the kitchen.

I looked across the cold steel bar and met my husband's eyes. "You were right." Only the night before, he'd wondered aloud if I had been abused as a child. I'd responded with vehement denial.

He stared into my eyes, and I returned a blank gaze. He knew what I meant.

"I have to leave."

"Okay."

"Mom and Dad are gone. I'm going to go to their house."

"Okay." Was he stunned, feeling helpless, or full of pity? I was too broken to figure it out, uncertain I even wanted to know.

I turned to the stairway. "Amber, you need to shower now so I can do your hair."

I picked up the phone and called my mother, who responded that I was welcome to stay at their condo. My sister, who lived a block away from her, had a key.

While Amber took her shower, I threw some things into a bag. Books. Movies. Licorice. Clothes.

I oiled and braided Amber's black hair with single-minded determination, intent on leaving as soon as possible. When I finished, I said goodbye, threw my bag in the car, and drove away.

On the freeway, I fought to keep the pressure on the gas pedal steady rather than push it to the floor and tear my way through the traffic.

I had to switch freeways, go through a canyon, and cross another valley to get to my mother's house. As the interchange drew closer, I fought the temptation to keep driving north to Canada.

In the canyon, a combination of curiosity, rebellion, and fear urged me to veer sharply off the road, but I forced the thoughts away and focused on the familiar route to my sister's apartment.

Marie opened the door to let me in. I moved in a dreamlike state, the edges of my vision fading to black as I looked down a long tunnel at my surroundings. Marie spoke, and I played the part of Dawn, though I wasn't sure who that was anymore. I said something, and Marie disappeared.

I was on a stage, not in a real house. Was I supposed to exit with her or stay? Uncertainty kept me there until she returned and stretched out her hand with a key in it.

Yes, the key. I needed the key to get into Mom's house.

Please don't ask.

In my distraction, I only caught the end of Marie's comment, ". . . come and see." I followed her to her daughter's bedroom.

"Isn't it cute?" she asked.

I stared blankly, not knowing what I was supposed to look at. "It's so cute." She turned away, and I followed her, clutching the key in my hand. It was my link to sanity, escape, and freedom.

She kept using unintelligible words, like the teacher in Peanuts, while I edged closer to the door, a frightened animal, unsure if I should remain still or bolt.

Marie paused, and I blurted, "I really need to go before I fall apart."

"Oh, okay."

I opened her door and closed it behind me before fleeing down the stairs. I drove to my parents' condo, unlocked the door, then locked it behind me. Alone, I sucked in a deep breath and tried to pretend I was simply on a pleasant getaway without the kids. I sat on the sofa in the living room, looked around the beautifully decorated open space, and jumped up. I couldn't be in that room. Instead, I walked around the kitchen and down the hall to the back room where the grandkids normally played. My mother's influence was heavy in this cozy room, and I relaxed.

Needing something to keep my hands busy, I pulled out a puzzle, but I couldn't focus. I was away from home, but I didn't know what to do. I lay down on the sofa and tried to absorb the change within me. I shifted positions, trying to get comfortable, but one word kept whirling around my head, slashing pain with every pass. *Molested.*

Exhaustion claimed me in sleep. When I woke, I decided to watch a movie. I padded into the living room, where my parents kept their DVD collection, and found one called *The Cokeville Miracle.* I'd never heard of it, but hoping it was truly something miraculous and would take my mind off my swirling thoughts, I grabbed it and carried it to the back room.

Soon the true story of children being held hostage at their elementary school by a crazed man with a homemade bomb unfolded. Parents panicked on-screen and pulled my torrent of emotions to the surface. Tremendous pain exploded from my chest and ripped through my body in a nightmare I couldn't wake from.

The most horrible thing that could happen to a child had happened to me. I hated violence to the point others made fun of me for not wanting to watch seemingly benign movies.

I returned to the puzzle, needing something to keep my mind and hands occupied. My stomach grumbled, but the thought of facing the world in search of food caused my anxiety to spike, so I put it off.

My cell phone rang. Assuming it was Chad, I picked it up without looking at the caller ID. "Hi, it's Ben. I was just calling to see if you needed anything." I rarely heard from my siblings, so Mom must have asked Ben to check on me.

"I don't want to leave to get some food, but I'm really hungry."

"I have some leftover roast and potatoes from dinner if you want that. It's still warm."

"That would be great. Thanks."

"We'll be over in about ten minutes."

"Okay."

I went to check my face in the bathroom mirror to make sure I didn't look horrible and was shocked to see an unfamiliar person. I'd lived in her skin for almost forty-one years. Did I even know who she was? I averted my eyes and left.

When the doorbell rang, I unbolted the door and let my brother and his wife in. I ate while we made awkward small talk. When I finished, they only lingered for a few minutes before reclaiming their dirty dishes and abandoning me to the solitude I craved.

I shuffled back to my cozy cocoon and stayed there until night swallowed day. I turned off the light and slept on the sofa, not bothering to climb in my parents' bed.

The next day I alternated between reading, watching television, and creating more drawings to try to understand what had happened to me. Then it was time to go home. My family needed me; I couldn't stay here forever. I packed my things, made sure everything was the way I'd found it, and climbed into my car.

A few days later, I met with Susan again. Before she even settled into her chair, I launched in. "I was sexually abused as a child."

"That doesn't surprise me. You have all the symptoms."

"I was doing nondominant-hand drawing. I even tried not to draw what I saw coming out. Since then, the memories are bubbling up on their own, I don't even need to do the nondominant-hand stuff."

"You didn't bring your drawings this time."

"No. There are too many. And I know what they mean." I continued. "It happened when I was eleven or twelve, but I was small and immature for my age. We played games like prince and princess. As the princess, I needed to kiss the frog—it was in all the storybooks. Once the frog was bad and jumped into my mouth. I didn't know then that the frog was a penis. How could I have?"

Susan shook her head.

"He collected girls' underwear, and he wanted to buy mine. I was poor and wanted the money, so I took it off and gave it to him, but he wanted another pair. I told him I only had one, but he groped around to make sure I wasn't hiding another pair. I don't know how long this all went on, but it wasn't a little while. I think it was a year or two."

Susan continued to listen patiently, so I kept going. "His mother walked into his room after he'd finished doing something to me. I remember being bare from the waist down, either with my skirt up or my pants off."

#memory

His mother looked at me and then at him. "What did you do?" she yelled.

"Nothing," he said while he did up his pants.

I sat frozen in place, too afraid to think of covering myself.

She turned to me. "What did he do?"

"Nothing," I said. She looked scary and mad.

"You put your underwear on and never take it off in front of a man again."

She turned to her son. "If I ever see something like this again, I'll slice it off myself." He left the room.

"You okay?" she asked sternly.

"Yes."

"Don't you ever tell anyone you took off your underwear or they'll think you're a whore. Didn't your no-good mother tell you not to do that?"

I continued to stare at her.

"If I ever hear a peep of this, I'll tell everyone what a tramp you are. You should be ashamed of yourself. Now get out and never come here again, you hear?"

I nodded and left.

I pulled out a memory my inner child had written about the encounter and read it to Susan.

Taking off underwear is bad. Good girls keep their clothes on, and I didn't, so I'm a bad girl. The lady said so. It wasn't the first time I took it off. He collects pretty underwear. Mine were really pretty. He said so, and I knowed so. I leaned back farther into the sofa, almost as if I wanted to stay away from the words I read. *I touched his dick, I did. Does that make me bad? We were playing a game. I was curious too. I wanted to know how it got so big. He even taught me about lady parts, but he had to show me, so I'd know what he was talking about. He was nice and was just teaching me. I was a good learner. I didn't know it was bad until the lady told me it was bad. I never went back. Ever. I stayed away from her at church too. And the man.*

I put the sheet away and looked up into Susan's understanding eyes. "How could she have done that to me?" I didn't wait for an answer. "I went home and told my mom, but I didn't have the words to make her understand. I told her I got yelled at by his mom for playing games. My mom even remembers our conversation."

I shook my head in frustration. "How did I not know this? All these years I had no memory that I was molested. It is the worst possible thing I can think of happening to anyone, and it happened to me. I want to deny it, but I can't. It's all true. I feel it, deep down."

"You know my story," Susan said. "I still don't remember most of my abuse. I remember before, and I remember after. Severe child abuse often becomes hidden. It's how we protect ourselves. We dissociate from what happened to the extent that we forget. It's called dissociative amnesia."

Dissociative amnesia. The word rolled around in my brain and finally settled. What if this discovery was only the tip of the iceberg?

Susan reached for a purple sheet of paper from a stack on her desk. "Our next AMAC group starts soon. I think it would be very helpful for you." I took the sheet and scanned the outline of topics for the Adults Molested as Children twelve-week course.

Susan had brought up the AMAC group before, but since I thought my abuse had been limited to my first marriage, I resisted going, as if I would be seen as a fraud for not having been abused as a child. Internally, the resistance remained. I wanted to stay hidden and pretend nothing had changed. Before I could talk myself out of attending, I said, "I'll be there."

11
WALKING ALONE

The flashbacks were surfacing daily now. I spun out of control, fearing the things hidden within me. Sometimes I wondered who the crazy person inside my head was because it couldn't be me. Not wanting others to see my brokenness, I spent as much time as possible in the safety of my home.

I continued to attend church but wasn't able to hold my emotions in. I often left in tears, but I persisted. As my anxiety rose, it brought with it an oppressive cloud of darkness. I needed to feel the calming influence of the Spirit.

One Sunday morning, things were particularly bad, but I fought through it for the hope of comfort I wanted to obtain at church.

I sat with my family, sang the hymns, and waited for the sacrament. As one of the priests began blessing the bread, I was suddenly no longer sitting in the pew as an adult but as a child listening to a different voice.

#flashback

The voice of my abuser floated over me from the speakers, surrounding me, as he blessed the bread that we might always remember Jesus Christ. When he finished, boys between twelve and fourteen picked up the trays of broken bread and walked to the pews. I sat near the aisle, and a boy in my Sunday School class stopped and held the tray out for me to take a piece.

I stared at the bread for a moment, not wanting to take something that had been blessed by someone who had hurt and betrayed me. But I had no choice; everyone would know I'd sinned if I didn't take the bread. My little hand stretched out and picked a piece up.

It tasted tainted, dirty, somehow. Was it because I had been told that what I'd been doing with the man was bad? Was I actually a sinner making things worse by unworthily taking the symbol of Christ's body? Was he pretending to be holy when he wasn't, or was I?

The confusion and revulsion of that moment washed over me as the flashback faded and reality came into focus. As an adult, I knew I wasn't a bad person. I hadn't sinned. The man whose name I didn't even know was the fraud. I glanced around, wondering if another abuser might be hidden in plain sight.

I crossed my legs, jiggling my right leg and chanting within my head, *This is about Jesus, not abusers.* I grasped a fidget toy my son no longer played with and worked the hard plastic between my fingers.

Behind me, a mother shushed a restless child. The bread was passed from one member of the congregation to another until it reached me. I looked at the harmless pieces of bread, but the revulsion from my flashback made me hesitate.

I took a piece and placed it in my mouth. It tasted like ordinary bread, and I reminded myself I wasn't that little girl anymore. Yet no matter how hard I forced my mind to return to the image of Jesus, the flashback played through my mind like a carousel I couldn't get off.

The water was being blessed now. With my eyes closed, I began mindlessly rocking back and forth. I stiffened my back to stop the motion, afraid it would betray all I carried inside.

When the blessing of the water ended, I tried to focus on the young men carrying the trays with tiny plastic cups. Water that had been blessed. Pure water.

#flashback

I sat in a hard metal chair with other young girls. The teacher was trying to help us understand chastity and how it related to purity.

"Think of it like gum. Once it's been chewed, no one wants it. It's still gum, but which would you rather have—a new stick or a piece someone has already chewed?"

I didn't squirm despite my shame. I stayed perfectly still so no one else would know I was a chewed-up piece of gum. My dream of a nice house, a husband, and happy kids had been shattered. No decent man would ever want me.

#flashback

Same hard metal chair, this time in a class of boys and girls. The teacher held up an old board with a few nails in it. "Sin is like putting nails into your board," he said. "The sins are hard

113

and stuck in place. Can you pull them out?" He gave each of us a try at tugging them out.

"Repentance is like this hammer; it takes the nails out of the board." Using the hammer, he pulled the nails out of the board with ease. Then he turned it so we could see the holes left behind. "It's always better not to sin in the first place so you aren't left with holes, but if we do, we can repent."

God forgave, but the scars remained.

I closed my eyes for a second and opened them again, wishing the flashbacks away. It wasn't only my abuser who'd hurt me; the teachers at church had hurt me too. The analogies they'd used were damaging. I carried those messages of worthlessness with me for years.

The tray of water hovered in front of me. How long had it been there? I pushed my feelings down and quickly drank the water, hoping I hadn't lost track of too much time. I passed the tray on down the row, reminding myself that with repentance there were no holes left behind; God wiped sin away as if it had never happened. But it had happened.

If God made the board new, why was I so broken? If he forgave and forgot, why was I remembering? Maybe he had forgotten but I remembered because I hadn't forgiven my abusers. The thought of forgiving them tasted bitter.

My thoughts rumbled from my head to my stomach. I forced myself to sit still until the sacrament was finished and the young men had sat down. Then I got up and left. I needed to run away from my flashbacks, my questions, and from anyone who might be pretending. There was no way I could tell the difference.

At home I wrapped myself in my blanket of isolation and attempted to still my racing thoughts. God had brought no justice to my abuser, who'd performed holy ordinances in public while privately abusing little girls at home. God had let people teach me that I was worthless, that I had been used, and that it was my fault.

Bits and pieces of other lessons surfaced. Girls needed to dress modestly so guys didn't turn to sin. Girls shouldn't be in places where bad things might happen. And most of all, good girls should always do what they were asked to do. Doing what I was asked to do was what had gotten me into this whole mess in the first place.

I turned on the television to drown out my thoughts, but it didn't help. I sat at my desk and opened a browser window where I typed, "signs of child abuse." I held on to the hope that somehow I was crazy and none of this had really happened, even though I knew it had. I didn't want to be that little girl.

I skipped over the signs for physical abuse; someone would have noticed bruises or burns, and I didn't remember anything like that. As I scrolled farther down, a list of general symptoms jumped out at me: sudden change in personality, withdrawing from others, self-harm or suicidal, abusive adult relationships, and chronic health problems as an adult. I had all of it. Even if I'd *only* been molested, I had all the symptoms. The evidence gave added weight to my discovery.

As I read on, I realized I'd been set up to fail. The predictor of future health problems was childhood abuse. Victims had a much higher risk of heart attack, stroke, and episodic paralysis—paralysis that came and went—like mine.

My paralysis.

No, I had no control over it. It wasn't in my head even if Dr. Smith hadn't been able to diagnose it. There was no way my paralysis was caused by being molested. I brushed aside thoughts of my paralysis and refocused on my discovery.

I wasn't crazy. I had all the symptoms of abuse. I had pages of drawings that I had actively tried not to create, yet they had poured out of me anyway. I had been molested as a child.

Once I accepted the truth of being abused, I needed to know how bad it was. The nondominant hand work might have initiated the memories, but now they came on their own. Eventually I was able to piece together enough details to ask my mother about who lived at the end of our lane in the home where the abuse happened.

Mom assumed it was Tony, a boy only a few years older than I was, but I quickly realized that wasn't right. This was someone old enough that I thought of him as a man, someone at least five years older.

As I explored deeper, I discovered it was an older boy in the same family. Tony's older brother, Kyle. The only problem was that in digging deeper, a new name surfaced. Jeff had also abused me.

While the kids were at school, I set out to discover who Jeff was. I got out my paper and colored pencils.

Across the top I wrote, *Who is Jeff?* with my right hand.

My left hand responded; *Jeff is bad like Carson. Jeff was older. I was fourteen and he could drive. He knew I lived in a shed. He picked me up at the end of the road. I felt sixteen until he raped me, and then I felt six.*

I began another page. If he raped me, I needed to know what had happened. Images emerged: Jeff and I smiling as he drove down the road, Jeff holding me down and raping me, then me alone in the dark with the words *stranded, pretend, alone,* and *broken* written across the page.

I wrote about how he'd left me on the side of the road to walk home alone. I drew a picture of him—muscular and strong with a king's crown . . . and blood dripping from fangs. Then I wrote, *Nice outside, devil inside.*

More words spilled out, horrible things this boy said to me. I sat back with more questions than answers. Memories rarely surfaced fully formed; rather, they came in fragments until I had enough that I was ready to accept the full memory. Sometimes I didn't even know what to believe until the memory surfaced completely. It could take minutes or weeks. In this case, it took three days.

#memory

Jeff was a popular football player and wrestler. At the end of the school year, he invited me to a party. I was the youngest in my class at fourteen, but I acted like I was sixteen—the magic age when Mormon kids were allowed to date. I'd have to sneak out, but the chance to hang out with the popular kids was too much to resist. Jeff was sixteen and could drive, so he planned to meet me at the end of our half-mile-long dirt lane.

I was sleeping in the shed next to our house at the time, so there wasn't much sneaking involved. I left a note on my bed just in case someone came looking for me, then shut my door and walked down the lane in my nicest T-shirt, jeans, and sneakers.

Jeff arrived at the promised time, and I climbed into his truck, the music blaring from his speakers slamming into me. Excitement bubbled up in me and showed up in a broad smile.

My friends would be jealous that I was going to a party with a football player.

At the crossroads, Jeff turned west rather than continuing north to town, but kids came from all over the rural area to go to school, so I wasn't alarmed. I'd never thought to ask where the party was.

Jeff slowed and pulled up in front of an old barn instead of continuing on to the party.

"Come on," Jeff said. "I want to show you something."

"Okay."

We walked into the barn, our footfalls muffled by the hay scattered across the floor. The shadowy hulks of old farm equipment peered out from both sides of the open space. Bits of light crept in through cracks in the walls and window openings. As I inhaled a combination of rust, dripping fluids, moldy hay, and dust, the first prickles that something wasn't right skittered up my spine.

Jeff walked over to the door, then back to me. "Why aren't you wearing a skirt?" He raked his hand through his blonde hair.

The question threw me. He was in jeans and hadn't told me anything about the party being something we needed to dress up for. Before I formed a response, he continued. "You need to change."

"I don't have anything to change into."

"Never mind."

"Didn't you want to show me something?"

"Yes." Jeff strode forward and kissed me hard as his arm snaked around my back.

I froze, my mind blank.

118

When he moved his hands to unbutton my pants, I took a step back, not knowing what do to.

"Don't be that way," he said. "I know you want me."

"*Want* you?" My voice was hushed with fear at his aggressive stance.

"Just take off your pants!" His anger pushed me another step backward, and I glanced past him at the door. He lunged forward and pushed me to the ground.

My arms shot out to cushion my fall and he was on top of me, yanking my pants down. I tried to scramble backward but made little headway, tangled up with him as I was. My pants caught on my shoes, and he shifted his weight as he turned to rip my shoes and clothes off, his muscles no match for my thin body, even if I'd tried to put up a decent fight. He turned back, straddled me, and grabbed my wrists with both hands. In one smooth motion, he moved them above my head and pinned them with one hand.

He looked me in the face, his eyes full of hatred. "Stop trying to get away, or I'll have to hurt you." He shifted position, using his free hand to unbutton his own jeans, and raped me quick and hard, his breath hot against my skin. My body stayed frozen in place, my eyes fixed on the rafters.

When he finished, he climbed off and did up his jeans. I remained in place, too scared to move.

"If you want a ride home, you better get dressed, 'cause I'm leaving." He turned and headed to the door.

"Are we going to the party?" I asked as I got up.

A bitter laugh escaped his lips as he turned back. "Like I'd ever take you to a party."

As he walked away, it occurred to me I had no idea where I was. If he left, I'd be lost.

119

I scrambled to untangle my pants and get them on. I zipped them up just as his door to his truck slammed. I grabbed my shoes and ran out the door as the engine roared to life. I jumped inside, and his tires skidded as he did a quick U-turn to head back the way we had come.

Though the music blared, he twisted the knob even higher. I clutched my shoes to my chest, in too much shock to put them on.

He didn't look at me or speak to me for the first five minutes. Mute tears wet my face, but I let them fall.

"You better not tell anyone about what happened." He slammed his hand against the steering wheel. "I mean it. Though it's not like anyone will believe you over me. Everyone in town hates Mrs. Thompson, and you along with her."

Confusion knit my brow. I didn't know why he was talking about Mom, who taught math and computers at the high school we attended.

"This is her fault." Jeff's voice was distant, like he wasn't talking to me anymore. "We're a team. If she messes with one of us, she messes with all of us. What did it matter to her anyway? He missed two games because she wouldn't listen to Coach and give him a passing grade."

I stayed silent and let him continue. "Everyone knows my family." His voice rose again, taking on a hard edge. "They won't believe a word from a pathetic loser like you. If you do tell, I'll screw your sister so hard she won't be able to walk for a week. And don't think I don't know about that scrawny little brother of yours. I could snap him like a twig."

His eyes left the road and rested on me. Whatever he saw caused him to cuss and hit the wheel harder. He slammed on the breaks, and the truck squealed to a stop. "Get out!"

I sat there looking at him, still paralyzed, my brain having stopped functioning.

"Get out of my truck!"

I climbed out and shut the door. Jeff spun his truck around and tore down the road away from me. Still clutching my shoes to my chest at the side of the road, I watched him disappear.

I automatically untied my shoes and dropped to the ground to put them on. I swiped at my face again and began walking the three miles home along the edge of the narrow country road. Dusk turned to darkness.

When I got to my lane, I turned and walked toward the lights of my house. I opened the door to the shed and curled in fetal position on my bed, crumpling the note I'd left beneath my body. I didn't cry.

12

I BREAK

B its and pieces of different memories continued to surface daily, leading me to realize there were multiple abusers—not one elusive man, not two or even three, but many.

The television played in the background while I frantically placed pieces within a puzzle in an attempt to cope while Chad tucked the kids into bed. I rocked back and forth, gaining speed until I was moving at a frenetic pace.

The pieces blurred. I looked at my arm and imagined taking a knife and, cutting deep, flaying my muscles open, blood pouring everywhere. I blinked away the vision.

No. I don't like pain.

The image refused to leave. It played in variations.

One tear became a flood, bringing with it sounds from the depths of my soul that burst forth. I'd never let my kids hear the ugly cry, but I had no control over it now.

When Chad returned, he quickly moved to my side. "What's wrong?"

"I don't know. Everything hurts."

He gently wrapped his arms around me while I sobbed and thought of all the knives in the house.

Ten minutes later, I was still out of control. The pain worsened, coming in waves that slammed into me, pushing me under as I struggled to stay above the surface.

"Can you have Stephen come over and help give me a blessing?"

"Sure," Chad said as he went to call Stephen.

Knowing Stephen would be arriving within minutes. I swallowed my emotions, refusing to let anyone see me broken.

As I went to the living room, I thought about using Chad's pocketknife but wondered how dirty it might be. I would find a clean knife to cut myself with after everyone fell asleep.

The doorbell rang, and Chad opened the door. He and Stephen talked for a minute while I sat hunched over, desperately trying to gain control. Lost in a world of pain, I couldn't comprehend their words.

They stood over me, placed a few drops of oil on my hair, then laid their hands on my head and began. I forced my sobs down until they finished, then doubled over in pain.

"Chad, you have to take me to the hospital," I cried in a pitiful voice I didn't recognize. "You have to keep me safe. Please."

"Okay, I'll take you right now."

While Chad left to get ready, Stephen sat down next to me. He rubbed my back a little, trying to offer any comfort he could. Oddly, it helped.

Amber appeared in the hallway, looking at me with concern. "What's wrong?"

Renewed pain tore through me, causing me to wail even harder. No child should see their mother like this.

Gavin joined Amber. "You okay, Mom?"

I choked down my emotions, trying to put a mask of reassurance on. I refused to make this any worse for them than it had to be. "Yes, I'm okay. I'm just sad. Daddy's going to take me to the hospital, and everything will be fine. Nicole will be here with you."

I turned to Chad, who had rejoined us. "Tell Nicole to come up and sit with them. They're scared."

I stood and went to my bedroom, where I packed toiletries, a few clothes, my phone charger, and a couple of books. Stephen was gone when I returned. Chad and I climbed into the van and drove to the hospital.

The twenty-minute ride allowed me to calm down. I sent a short text to Chad's mother letting her know I was fine and asking her to take care of Chad while I was in the hospital. She offered to go to the house, but I knew the kids were asleep and with their older siblings. We arrived at the hospital shortly after 10:00 p.m. All the emotion had died, but not my obsession with cutting my arms. A shell that looked like me walked into the emergency room. The real me avoided physical pain and hospitals.

"I need to check my wife in."

"What are we checking her in for?"

"I want to cut my arms up," I responded in monotone.

We sat down and waited. Sick people surrounded me, but I wasn't sick. I was crazy.

A nurse called my name, and I followed her to a square room with a blue plastic bed bolted to the floor and a blue plastic chair with no sharp edges. Chad and I answered a few questions, and she left, instructing me to change into a hospital gown. I did so, and other people came, asked questions, and left. The night slipped by.

A nurse sat outside my door, keeping tabs on me to make sure I didn't turn into a screaming lunatic, but I lay there quietly, wondering how this had happened to me.

I tossed with troubled sleep, where a shadowy man buried beneath my amnesia peeked through the rubble. Not a man. A monster.

I woke with a start. *Who are you? What else did you do to me?* I needed to know as much as I wanted to forget. It was this man's fault I wore a flimsy hospital gown instead of my own clothes.

"When is the social worker going to be back?" I asked Chad. He was leaning against the wide doorway instead of using the ugly plastic chair.

"I don't know." Worry coated his voice. He walked over, sat near me on the low bed, and rested his hand on my shoulder. His warmth seeped through the numbness, offering me the comfort I so desperately craved.

"What time is it?" I asked.

Chad pulled out his phone. "Almost two in the morning."

Four hours in this bleak room. Several scuffs on the floor testified of the violence some patients had exhibited here, but the cavalry stayed away. The squeak of shoes on linoleum got louder and then faded down the hall while the fluorescent lights above beat against my eyelids. I wanted to sleep, but when I closed my eyes, I saw knives piercing the translucent skin of my arm until a long, deep gash opened. Others would witness the depths of pain hidden inside me, colored deep red.

The monsters from my past had brought this craving with them. It was their fault, and I hated them. I had no desire to die. Perhaps I could give in to the craving a little by dragging a knife shallowly along my arm.

I rolled over and grasped Chad's hand. Warmth seeped up my arm, like holding a mug of hot cocoa, as I clung to my anchor, my life preserver, and my reason for living. Time became abstract as the minutes swirled and danced to their own beat.

"Hello," a cheerful voice suddenly chirped. The social worker had returned. "There are no beds in the Salt Lake Valley. We can send you to Ogden or Provo. Which would you prefer?"

Suddenly she became the object of my hate. Chipper birds like this didn't belong here. She couldn't understand my darkness, even suggesting earlier that I go to a hotel instead of the hospital, but I knew I'd find a way to hurt myself there.

"Ogden," I said.

"It's closer to where we live," added Chad.

"Okay, I'll get started on the paperwork."

"Will I be able to drive her?"

"No, she'll have to go by ambulance. It's hospital policy."

"Okay, thanks."

She slipped away with steps that made no sound. Was she a finch or a robin? No, an annoying scrub jay.

I looked at Chad's posture. He was exhausted. "You should go home and get some sleep."

"I'd stay, but I have work tomorrow and I've got the kids. Are you sure you'll be okay?" He looked torn, helpless, and upset.

What did "okay" mean anymore? The crazy-town carousel was spinning at full tilt, the seat belt the hospital was providing ensuring I didn't fly off. "I'm going to try to get some sleep. I'll be fine."

"Okay. I'll see you tomorrow." Chad gently kissed me and walked out the door. I missed him even before his footsteps faded away. I wanted to scream at him to come back, but I knew the kids needed an adult at home with them and he needed to go to work. We'd learned to rely only on ourselves, and that meant we often faced things alone. I trusted he would be taken care of because of the text I'd sent his mother.

I worked on shutting everything out. I locked away my worries about the kids, my loneliness, and my fear that I was crazy. I convinced myself I wasn't freezing in the cold hospital room and that I wasn't exposed in my thin hospital gown. I reminded myself the heavy door without a knob on the inside would never close to trap me inside as long as I stayed calm and quiet for the nurse who sat in the hall.

After tucking myself as tightly as I could into the thin blankets, I closed my eyes and listened intently to the low hum of hospital machinery until exhaustion claimed me.

Something woke me up. I must be cold. Yes, I was cold, but that wasn't it. I opened my eyes. The nurse stationed outside my door was handing papers to a tall man in a dark uniform.

"She's pretty docile. You shouldn't have any problems," she said. I'd never been described as docile before.

A stocky paramedic came into view with a yellow gurney. *No problems here, at least not for you.*

"This is my fourth transport to McKay Dee the last couple days." The tall guy grumbled to the nurse. "I might as well have been assigned there."

The stocky guy set the brake on the gurney and smiled reassuringly at me. "Do you need help getting on the gurney?" he asked.

"No, I can do it." My voice sounded normal. Weird.

I tried not to flash too much flesh while I climbed on in my gown, wishing again for my own clothes. Sitting up in the comfortable gurney was nice, like my own stroller. The gentle giant tucked in my blankets and strapped me in. With the bands snug against me, I felt safe for the first time.

The two men rolled the gurney down the corridors and out into the dark. Not morning yet. My gurney was placed into a dark metal box, and the doors clanged shut with finality, like the lid to a casket at the end of the viewing. I reminded myself it was just an ambulance.

With barely a shudder, we were on our way, the hospital on the other side of the tiny back windows shrinking as we moved forward. I watched shadowy buildings and streetlights outside move past until dizziness forced my eyes closed.

The memory of my last ride in an ambulance, physically paralyzed instead of mentally paralyzed, flashed in my mind. I thought of the bumpy road the bad shocks couldn't mask, the paramedic holding my hand between his legs to put in an IV on our way to a different hospital. All I'd wanted was to open my eyes and see what an ambulance looked like on the inside.

I opened my eyes and looked around. Everything about this ambulance was new. The comfortable gurney, the glossy maroon cabinets, the gleaming silver handles. No evidence of life-and-death struggles here.

Above me, a dim light shone through the sparkling plastic that encased it. I let the light watch over me and looked out the back window again.

The stocky paramedic ducked in from the front and sat on the maroon vinyl bench beside me with a clipboard. He silently filled out paperwork while I returned to staring at the night-light above me.

Thank you for sitting with me, I wordlessly said to him.

When my eyes began watering, I closed them, and scenes flashed across the backs of my eyelids: Dark-chocolate eyes wide with fear when my howls of pain had pulled my daughter from bed. The crease of worry etched on Chad's forehead. The stick figures I'd drawn doing unspeakable things. The sick games I played with my abuser. Abusers, I reminded myself. Kyle wasn't the only one.

The shadowy man from my nightmares climbed his way to my awareness. He wanted to be known as much as I wanted answers to the questions that refused to let me rest. How often had I been abused? How long had it continued? What else had happened to me? The questions overwhelmed me, so I opened my eyes and concentrated on the night-light in an attempt to block everything out.

The ambulance exited the freeway. In my numbness, the forty-five-minute drive had flown by. More shadowy buildings and wisps of trees made me feel disoriented. I was hopelessly lost until the glowing hospital signs shone brightly through the windows—a lighthouse to guide my way.

The ambulance backed up to the building and stopped. The paramedics pulled my special stroller out, the legs clicking into place before the wheels quietly took over. I glided through a set of double doors and down several long halls.

Words floated back and forth between the two paramedics and their hospital guide with the special badge that turned the locks from red to green, but they ignored me. Did I even exist? Was I somewhere deep inside this crazy person who wanted to slash her arms?

The hospital staff cataloged my bag of possessions, only letting me keep two paperback books. No curling iron, electronics, or even my Chapstick. I never went anywhere without Chapstick. They took my clothes, even my underwear, and gave me disposable underwear and two gowns, one worn backward, to cover myself. They took my clothes to wash them, even the clean ones I'd packed.

I followed a female nurse to a shared room where she handed me a new set of earplugs. "Since you were in the ER all night, we'll let you get some sleep," she said.

"What time is it?"

"It's six thirty in the morning."

I was a light sleeper, rarely slept during the day, and hated earplugs. I put the earplugs in and went to sleep anyway. As it turned out, psych wards are not made for restorative sleep. They are made to keep people safe. Someone checked on me every fifteen minutes. People came in to take my vitals and ask questions, which forced me to remove the earplugs. I fell asleep in between their visits and got what rest I could until a male nurse interrupted me to ask if I wanted to come out for lunch.

"Yes," I replied.

He moved over to the other bed. "It's lunchtime. You going to come eat?"

"I'm not eating when you disrespect it by spitting on it!" A rude voice burst out from a tangle of sheets, blankets, and dark, wavy hair.

I decided to ignore it and headed to the bathroom. The door covered about half the doorway, allowing someone to see over the top and under the bottom. The tops of everything in the room sloped. It made sense that there wasn't a place to perch on top of the shelves that held our stuff, but why was the top of the door slanted?

I padded into the empty, tiled space. The only soft thing was a small hand towel. I relieved myself and helplessly watched a spider crawling across the floor. I had no shoes, nothing hard to kill it with. I realized I didn't care. I pushed a button above the toilet to flush it, walked past the spider, and pushed another button over the sink. Water splashed on my hands, so I knew this was real despite the numbness inside.

In the common area, I picked up my tray of food and sat at a table across from a guy covered in scabs from an extreme-sports accident. I ate my hamburger while he rambled on, and left as soon as possible. He was crazy to endanger his life as if it didn't matter.

Back in my room, I discovered my clothes had been returned, folded neatly in a blue plastic crate. I changed, happy to feel something familiar.

I didn't want to share space with the rude bundle, so I grabbed a book and walked out to the common area, which was the center of our pod.

Our unit was one of eight psychiatric pods split into two units each. A circular nurses' station in the center allowed for the supervision of both units. The common area consisted of a ring around the nurses' station, with locked doors preventing us from going to the other unit where more broken people resided. The shared rooms curved along the edges of the pod, doors facing inward.

I sat down on a vinyl sofa, opened my book, and read the same paragraph several times. The people were too distracting. A young woman rocked and paced while a forty-something boasted loudly about how the police almost tased him. I looked around, noticing that the women were more likely to have vacant eyes while the men cried, opposite from outside.

I wanted out of here. I hated feeling locked in, and I didn't like the oppressive feeling. I needed to figure out how to get myself out. Though I looked back at my book, I was listening and thinking. One nurse reported to another that someone had refused to attend groups and she needed to cooperate or she couldn't leave.

From then on, I did everything asked of me. I ate the food they put in front of me and attended every group: Tai Chi in the common area, Apples to Apples with the rec therapist, group therapy with a counselor.

I watched an old man lie constantly and make a nurse cry on her first day. He didn't want to leave the unit. I wondered how horrible his life on the outside must be for him to want to be in here.

I met with doctors and answered their questions. That night at dinner I stared at the wide, round spoon next to my piece of chicken and green salad. The guy across the table from me had pork chops, with a similar round spoon. Apparently forks were too dangerous, so, like an infant, I struggled to eat my food with the oversized spoon.

My husband and daughter arrived during the short visiting hour. I drank them in and longed for home, where I belonged. When they left, they took my peace with them. There was no air in this cage. I hid from the other patients in my room only to find my roommate in the shower singing in a different language and periodically screaming. Her shower ran on and on until the room filled with steam.

I took the opportunity to change into my pajamas and kept reading, my only escape. At bedtime, I turned off my light and lay staring at the ceiling. My roommate began sharing strange stories of protecting her bible from curses and from the ghosts that taunted her. Eventually, she fell into a fitful sleep, but I was wide awake, surrounded by the dampened energy of despair and hopelessness that soaked the walls.

Heat radiated back at me from the plastic bed in a room still muggy from hot steam. Fluorescent light from the window on the door assaulted my eyes, and the noise of the nurses talking and laughing grated on my ears. I gave up on sleep, grabbed a book, and went out into the cool air to sit on a plastic sofa with rounded edges. I escaped to a world where a young woman caught the eye of a duke who saved her from a life of drudgery.

Movement caught my eye. Another spider, a little bigger, crawled across the vinyl toward me. I slammed my book down on it, spreading spider guts on my book, shocked that I didn't care. When my eyes grew blurry, I returned to bed.

The next morning, I ate pancakes and eggs with my spoon. I knew I hadn't been eating much, and it surprised me how a break from the stress at home and regular food had revived my sanity.

Today was my forty-second birthday, and I wanted to go home. When it was my turn to meet with the doctor, I explained how I had gotten to this place, how my need to cut myself was gone, and how I would cope when I got home. After ten minutes, he agreed to send me home. I kept calm, but I wanted to rush the door and demand it open to let me out.

A few hours later, I finished my second book, still waiting for the paperwork to be processed. Not long after, Chad arrived, and they let us sit together in a room as we waited.

Finally, they handed me my possessions and unlocked the door. Gripping Chad's hand, I walked outside. The sun hit my skin, followed by a hot breeze. I looked at the trees with their fluttering leaves and marveled at how my shoes protected my feet, softening the blows on the pavement. I let go of Chad's hand long enough for him to unlock the car door and for both of us to climb in and then grasped it again. I arrived home to find everything clean and quiet.

"Your Mom picked Amber and Gavin up right before I left to pick you up. They'll stay up there until Sunday night."

Four days of quiet. I went to the bedroom, set my stuff down, then soaked up the comfort of my own bed. I had just gotten up to get a glass of water when Nicole walked in with her grandma, holding a bakery box. She smiled and handed it to me.

I opened the lid to see a beautiful chocolate cake nestled inside, declaring, "Happy Birthday, Dawn!"

My eyes welled with tears. I set the cake down and gave my daughter and then my mother-in-law a hug. "Thank you."

I hadn't been forgotten. It was my birthday, and people cared about me. Best of all, I wasn't in the psych ward, I was alive, and I was home.

13

FINGERPRINTS

It wasn't long before the pain began coming in waves and the anger shattered my fragile sense of peace. I wanted to destroy the men who had abused me. I wanted them to experience my pain even though I knew it wasn't Christian to feel that way.

I kept going to therapy. It helped, but it was like trying to clear up a mudslide with a hand trowel. Anyone who got close got covered in mud as well. I kept people at a distance, especially my in-laws, after finding out they had let Chad struggle alone while I was in the hospital, even after I'd asked his mother to take care of him.

As my mental health declined, I withdrew from even Chad. I had nothing to give—no energy to help others, work out family problems, or face additional stress.

My abusers had left their fingerprints all over my life, molding my likes and dislikes, creating fears and destroying boundaries. I couldn't figure out where they stopped and I began. Who was I?

I pulled out a notebook and made a list of anything that was only me. I wrote Painting. What I painted indicated the trauma of my past, but my love of painting had nothing to do with what had happened to me.

Singing. Though it explained why I suddenly stopped singing at home.

My faith in God. I was angry at God, but that proved I believed in him. I also knew he would love me no matter how angry I was.

My mind went blank, but writing down even those three items helped me gain a sense of identity. If I could expel the abusers from my soul, I could build on those blocks.

Because the flashbacks continually assaulted me, I stopped going to church. I stayed away from extended family gatherings. Too weak to pretend or cope with the discomfort I caused, I stayed home, where I was safe, and focused on getting through each exhausting day. On the rare days I had a bit of energy, my kids were first in line.

I felt physical sensations of the abuse and wondered if I were going completely crazy. It started with the impression of two hands on my rear end. My visual or auditory flashbacks came and left, but this lingered for days, until I decided I needed another round of EMDR, or eye movement desensitization and reprocessing, similar to what I had done to heal from the abuse of my first marriage. I dreaded the process, but I didn't know what else to do.

I had discovered that my first therapist hadn't followed appropriate protocol, probably because EMDR was still fairly new then. I found a woman with twenty years' experience who specialized in EMDR and women's issues. I made an appointment and steeled myself for the darkness.

Chad tried to be reassuring, but I could tell he was nervous about it as well. We both worried about what new horrors we would surface.

My new therapist talked about targeted therapy. I needed to choose a flashback, identify the associated negative or irrational thoughts, then hold that image in my mind with a positive truth to rewire my brain while her fingers tapped back and forth on my knees.

We started with the flashback bothering me the most—the phantom hands that had held me captive for the past five days. We went through the therapy, and immediately the sensation disappeared.

Next, I targeted the feeling of a penis on my cheek and the taste of brownies associated with it. That sensation was inconsistent, but I wanted it gone. It also disappeared.

I saw my inner child. As she raged and cried, I told her it wasn't her fault. My therapist interrupted me to see how I was doing.

"My inner child is furious. I am trying to comfort her."

"Okay, let's keep going."

I had no idea what to do with the amount of sadness and anger she radiated. I only knew that the anger needed somewhere to go. Kyle stood in front of me, taller than I was, with brown hair. My inner child flew at him in a rage. She punched and kicked him with all her might, but she was small and weak, and it didn't affect him. Then she and I merged.

With my adult size and strength, I beat him with a ferocity I'd never experienced. A small part of me cowered at my uncontrolled anger, but not enough to stop me. Instead, I slowed down the motion and savored it. My muscles contracted in a kick to his ribs, my foot connected, and the air rushed out of his lungs. I savored the visceral sensations of every punch landing, not on some phantom in my head but as if on a real person. I held on to a thread of knowledge that I wasn't actually hurting anyone, which allowed me to enjoy it without guilt or consequences.

I stopped and looked down at him, curled and bleeding at my feet. If I continued, he would die. I stepped back, and a nurse stepped forward to help him. I turned away from the broken body and saw my husband standing there. I took his hand and started to walk away.

Chad squeezed my hand and said, "If it had been me, I would have killed him."

I laughed, and we left together. I knew I didn't want to kill him, but I did need to fight back. I needed to release my anger and frustration.

I opened my eyes to the gloomy office, feeling lighter and better than when I'd arrived. I'd beat a man to within an inch of his life, and it felt shockingly good. The best part was I wasn't going to jail for it.

I'm sure EMDR is as different for each person as their unique brain and problems. I let go, and my mind did what it needed to do.

In that moment, I knew I had changed. If someone attacked me, I would fight. A perpetrator would have to kill me before I'd let him hurt me again, and I'd make sure to leave plenty of forensic evidence.

A few weeks later, at what turned out to be my final session of EMDR, I brought a picture I had drawn with my nondominant hand. I'd asked what I needed to work on and ended up with three drawings across the page: a stick figure representing Kyle surrounded by a large red circle with a line across it; a broken, bleeding heart; and finally, a sad face with tears running down the page. I needed to ban my abuser from my life, heal my broken heart, and stop the pain.

We began with the first item: getting rid Kyle. I held the picture in my head and let go of control.

In my mind, I held a worn-and-blurry photograph of my abuser in my left hand. I hadn't seen Kyle for almost thirty years. From slightly behind and off to my right, a bright light shone and landed on the photograph. I knew it was the healing power of God. Little spots appeared on the photo. The spots blackened, expanded, and eventually disintegrated the image into bits of ash that blew away until there was nothing left, the ghost that had haunted my life permanently gone.

I turned to the ocean of tears my sadness had created. I saw my twelve-year-old self facing Kyle's mother, who'd shamed me into staying quiet and forgetting the abuse. I yelled at this woman while she stood there and absorbed it. Eventually I stopped, realizing that I needed to listen to her instead.

She was there, in my mind, as if her spirit were visiting me. She communicated not in words as much as in feelings that said, "I'm sorry. I was dealt a shock I didn't know how to deal with. I didn't mean the things I said to you, I had no idea what to do or say. No mother expects or wants to see what I saw. I denied the truth.

"Over the years I worried about you. I am happy you moved on, met a wonderful man, and have a beautiful life. I'm grateful you have been healed.

"I'm so sorry I hurt you. Please forgive me."

I forgave her, and peace descended on us both, then a tiny ray of light drew her back to heaven.

I turned to my child self and hugged her. I missed her inno-cent joy in my life. I missed her play, her smile, her silliness. I loved her and wanted her just the way she was. The light that filled her eyes with hope and joy was beautiful to see. In that moment, she merged with me, fully integrated into my adult self.

Only one picture remained: my broken, bleeding heart. My therapist and I began again. In all my other visualizations, I'd stood next to my inner child, helping her, but now my child self and my adult self were integrated. I stood alone, unsure what to do, exposed and uncomfortable.

Knowledge washed over me. The shock and pain I'd expe-rienced as an adult in realizing what had happened to me as a child had broken my heart. The cracks had deepened as I under-stood how the abuse had affected my life and my children's lives. I looked down. My heart lay in my hands, not a representative shape but my true and beating broken heart.

A white finger showed me a long gash in my heart. It needed to be fused through the power of God. I saw the result would be a whole and complete heart, not even a scar showing. It ended with a feeling of questioning. Did I want my heart to be healed? Yes. I gave my consent.

I did not see the angel, but he was there. He began by using the power of his priesthood to bless me. I marveled at his words. His white finger hovered over the bottom of my heart, then slowly moved up the break, fusing it. Every part of the abuse—the pain, the anger, and lingering effects—was wiped clean. I emerged reborn.

When I walked out of the office, I remembered only the first phrase of the words the angel had blessed me with. While I don't remember the rest, the power remained. I had been healed and blessed by God through an angel. I knew that whatever came next, God would be there to help me through it. Clinging to him was my only hope to heal completely.

14

EMPTY BOX

It seemed every time I conquered one trial, another rose in its place. My family prided themselves in their independence to the point of only seeing each other at weddings, funerals, and every other Thanksgiving. I rarely chatted with my siblings over the phone or even through email. Chad's family, on the other hand, gathered at every holiday and on Sundays. Chad and I called ourselves the black sheep of his family until I finally realized that we were so different we weren't the black sheep, we were llamas. Communication was the biggest problem, and I'm sure I caused as many hurt feelings as I received. I'd learned to stay quiet and closed off around them to avoid being hurt but attended the gatherings for Chad's sake.

Things were stable until one of Chad's sisters, Lisa, moved back to Utah after living out of state for years. I didn't know her or have a relationship with her, but she thought she knew me from keeping in touch with her family and hearing their side of our interactions. I'd been in a Mexican standoff for years. Lisa ushered in the cold war.

Everything came to a head when her husband hounded my daughter about some recent medical symptoms until she was in tears. I let people hurt me, but not my kids. My daughter hadn't given her uncle all the information about her various medical problems because she felt it was personal. As an oncologist, he knew her symptoms didn't match up with the few things she'd told him, and he'd pushed the issue, insisting she needed better medical care, while she went into a full-blown anxiety attack. I wasn't there, and no one intervened to help her. When I found out, I overreacted—another side effect of dealing with the abuse.

I called Lisa to ask if I could drop off a note for her husband. I wrote numerous drafts until I was able to keep the note neutral, letting him know we were giving our daughter adequate medical care and she didn't have to share all her medical issues because it was her business and not his.

Lisa and I both went into full-blown mother-bear mode.

"No, you can't drop a note off," Lisa said. "You get offended easily, and then you send mean emails."

There was only one mean email I'd sent thirteen years earlier. My father-in-law, Todd, tended to put his foot in his mouth at times. I was always assured that he didn't mean it, but it didn't stop the hurt.

We were living in Wisconsin when he'd come to attend my son's baptism. In my home, it was harder to keep my emotional armor in place. Looking back, I know that his comments showed a lack of understanding rather than judging or trying to hurt me, but at the time, I was suffering from severe depression and anxiety and saw everyone as a threat.

After he left, I knew I couldn't allow him into my safe space ever again. I sent him an email where I tried to stand up for myself against what I saw as his attacks on me over the years as well as the recent one in my own home. I went too far and told him he was not welcome in my home because I needed to feel safe there.

Three days later, my mother-in-law, Pam, called. She told me Todd had cried for three days over what I had said. She let me know how much I had hurt him and that he'd never meant to hurt me with the things he'd said.

I prayed until I got to a place where I could give a sincere apology and hurried and called him. I apologized, trying to patch things up, and got off the phone. But he never apologized, and my hurt remained.

How did Lisa even know about the email? It confirmed that my in-laws were talking about me behind my back. That email had nothing to do with Lisa.

"I only did that once, thirteen years ago. I learned it wasn't a good thing to do, so I never did it again. When we moved back from Wisconsin, Judy didn't talk to me for a year, and I had no idea why. It was years before I figured it must have been that email. I still don't know for sure."

Things only went downhill from there. If Lisa was going to tell me I was mean, I might as well let out my pent-up hurt. I went off on her, she defended her family against me, and I got off the phone in tears.

As I cried to my husband, I found out that Lisa had called him to apologize for her husband's behavior to our daughter. It was then that I found out that apologies never come directly from the people involved; they moved around the family like notes passed in class. It took me over twenty years of marriage to finally understand that piece. Pam, my mother-in-law, was the only one who'd ever tried to discuss anything directly with me. She was also the one who'd apologized for Todd, which was why he never did.

My therapist and I talked often about the struggles I had interacting with my in-laws and the rejection and pain I felt. Susan counseled me often to cut off contact with them, but I didn't want to hurt anyone.

When I walked into my next therapy session, I noticed that the butterfly mobile that had sat on her desk for the past year now hung from the ceiling. Everything in Susan's office held meaning and purpose.

"Your mobile is up."

"I grabbed one of the tall therapists and had him help me hang it."

"Now you have to tell me what it means."

"What happens if one butterfly tries to fly away?"

"It wouldn't be able to. It's attached to the mobile."

"But what happens to the other butterflies if it tries to fly away?"

I gazed in thought for a moment. "They're attached, so if one tries, it will throw off the balance and cause the others to move." I thought of the immense energy required for that butterfly to even try.

"And then the other butterflies would pull the one back. People don't like change. It makes them uncomfortable. They hold back the one who is trying to move forward so that they can return to where they are comfortable."

Susan stayed quiet while I thought of those pulling at me to stay silent and pretend to be what they wanted. "How can the butterfly progress if it can't get the others to move as well?" We both knew we were really talking about my relationship with my in-laws.

"You can't force others to change."

I sagged in defeat. "So I just have to accept things the way they are."

"That's one choice. How else could that butterfly fly away?"

I gazed at the beautiful blue butterfly. I snipped the cord binding it, and it fluttered away, free to be itself instead of chained to others. "Someone would have to detach it and set it free."

"You have to cut the ties to those who want to hold you back. It is their choice to stay where they are but your choice to stay or progress."

Staring at that mobile, I made a choice. I had to fly, even if it meant cutting connections and leaving others behind. I'd spent years pushing out of my cocoon to become a butterfly. Now I refused to live only half alive, tethered to others' fears and expectations. I chose right then to cut off all contact with my in-laws.

Susan and I talked about the recent conversation with my sister-in-law and how it had hurt me.

"It's time to cut off contact with them," I said.

Susan nodded.

I expected freedom and excitement, but sadness washed over me. It was hard to leave the other butterflies.

My holiday season changed. I made my own Thanksgiving dinner for my family with all our favorite dishes. Most of our Christmas traditions were tied to my in-laws, and I missed the parties and get-togethers. The holiday spirit fled as flashbacks triggered by the season plagued me, causing my anxiety to rise, along with depression.

The fragmented pieces of my flashbacks formed a picture I didn't want to look at—until the symptoms of avoiding it became worse than the cure. I sat down for the easy part, drawing, which happened in the childlike part of my brain that didn't judge, merely observed. It was the shock of discovery, internalizing the event, and coping with the issues around it that were difficult.

I focused on my task until I saw the whole picture, then stared at the pages I'd drawn and written. No wonder I struggled with Christmas this year.

Thirty years ago, I had ruined Kyle's Christmas because he'd attempted to have intercourse with me; I'd clenched my body and lay stiff on the bed. He hadn't forced his way in, but it had made him angry.

#memory

Kyle grabbed my throat and thrust his face toward mine before he remembered not to leave any marks. He abruptly let go.

I stared, wide-eyed. I hated it when my secret boyfriend acted scary.

"You haven't been a good girlfriend, but you can make it up to me," Kyle said. "I want to buy you something for Christmas, but if I do, I won't have any money left to get my friends stuff. If you can come to my party and be nice to my friends, I'll tell them that is my gift, and then I can give you something nice."

The carrot dangled in front of me. I got little attention at home and even fewer gifts. I needed to show him I was a good girlfriend, so I agreed.

The day of the party arrived. Kyle, his brother Tony, two of Kyle's friends I'd never met before, and a neighbor boy around my age were the guests. I was the entertainment.

Kyle stood next to me as I sat on a chair. "No sex. She's mine." He looked at the others. "But we can have lots of other fun."

I was the only girl, the center of the attention. I played my part well, laughing and letting the boys do whatever they wanted to. Tony was first, then he pushed the neighbor boy to take his turn, but he refused. Rejection from the cutest boy stung, so I lavished my attention on the next boy, Skinny.

"Come on, Skinny, it's time to learn to be a man." Bandit said. Despite the prodding, Skinny did little and quickly moved back to observe.

Then came Bandit, the oldest of the bunch, a burly boy with a mean glint in his eyes. He made sure I never heard his real name and bragged to the other guys that he loved to rape girls. I'd never heard the term before, but I knew it was bad. He was rough and aggressive. I masked my pain and tension with a smile for Kyle, willing Bandit to finish.

Finally, it was Kyle's turn. As my boyfriend, he had expectations and rights the others didn't. The other boys enjoyed the show as they egged us on and drank their sodas.

Kyle zipped up his pants and grabbed a cardboard box sitting off to the side. It held no wrapping, but I didn't care. I eagerly opened the flaps and looked inside.

I stared at the bottom of an empty box. I looked up in confusion while the guys laughed.

"As if I'd waste my money on you," Kyle said.

I finally figured out that they were laughing at me; me and my empty box.

"Without any boobs, you're not even worth the price of a cheap whore," Bandit said.

Whore was another word that confused me, but I shoved it aside. I heard the message loud and clear. Something inside me broke.

The boys filed out. The last one was Skinny, who looked at me with compassion, reached into his pocket, and pulled out a quarter. He held it out, and I took it. I looked down at the quarter in my hand as Skinny left.

Kyle had lied to me and laughed at me. I felt empty, worthless, and ugly.

Their cruel laughter echoed in my ears all those years later. My heart broke like a glass ornament shattering in slow motion on a hard floor, scattering shards of pain. As an adult, I experienced their cruelty again, this time with an understanding I didn't possess as a child. It resonated through my entire body. I curled into a fetal position, then twisted away, unable to sit still, unable to process, unable to cope.

I needed Mom, but I knew she was driving to Idaho to visit my brother. Even if her cell phone had reception, she was busy. I ran for the bathroom, clutching my stomach. My body was trying to eject the pain with my breakfast.

I pulled out a puzzle and settled on the bed to try to calm myself. The television drowned out the voices in my head while I focused on the colored pieces. An hour later, the phone rang, and I picked it up off the nightstand.

"Hi, it's Pam. How are you doing?"

"I'm okay."

"All morning the Spirit kept telling me I needed to call you."

Relief flooded through me. Mom wasn't available, but my mother-in-law was here as the second mother she'd always wished to be, and right when I needed her.

She continued. "I want my whole family together today, and you are part of my family. It won't be the same without you."

I closed my eyes. It wasn't because I needed her; it was because I'd refused to attend the Christmas party. I stayed quiet.

"I don't know all of what has gone on, and I don't want to. You need to let it go. I don't know how much longer I have left. This might be our last Christmas together."

The pain I'd pushed down over the last hour came roaring to the surface, adding with it the pain my in-laws had caused. I tried to keep her from hearing, but there was no way to stop it. It was my fault again. I countered the blame by internally raging that she would bring up her fears of dying to pressure me into attending.

"My daughters aren't perfect, but they love you. Out of all of them, Judy is the most selfless, kind, loving person I know. She would never intentionally hurt you."

More proof they'd continued to talk about me, or Pam wouldn't have brought up what Lisa and I had talked about.

"She didn't speak to me for a year, and I never knew why," I exclaimed. "I figured it had to be because of the email I sent Todd. I called her this week to apologize, even though it had nothing to do with her, and she admitted that was the reason she hadn't talked to me."

Despite my inability to mask my crying, Pam continued to talk about the party and how it wouldn't be the same without me there.

"I have to go," I choked out. I hung up before she could say anything more.

Flashes of memories from the past twenty tumultuous years dealing with my in-laws began to batter me. It didn't matter what

I did. I was different, and I was wrong every time. Judy continued to show up to Sunday dinners every week for a year while ignoring me, yet somehow she was loving and selfless and I was the mean one? I curled back into a fetal position and urged Chad to take the kids and leave me alone.

Christmas came and went with little fanfare. I was coping, but my pain and anger consumed me. The emotions weren't new to me, but their intensity was. Caught in the storm, I bobbed in a life raft surrounded by an ocean of pain that threatened to drown me at any moment. Chad stood safely on shore, willing to help but unable to find me.

15

THROWING EGGS

Despite not wanting to attend the Adults Molested as Children group, I'd made a commitment, so I got in my van, drove down to the building, and walked inside. I sat in the closest folding chair, away from the couches that formed two sides of the U-shaped arrangement. I cautiously checked out the other women in our small group, surprised that they looked normal, like any of the faceless people I walked past while running errands.

My therapist, Susan, was facilitator. Introductions were made and rules laid out. Typical first-meeting stuff. My anxiety was high, but I made it through the first meeting.

In the second and third meetings, we reviewed many of the things I'd heard from my therapist, and I was able to contribute to the group about ways I'd implemented the strategies. Group was interesting, but I wasn't sure what I was going to get out of it.

The fourth week, we started to share our stories. One by one we opened up and transformed from a group of women to a band of sisters. Beginning at a horribly young age, these beautiful women had all been abused by brothers, uncles, babysitters, and neighbors.

I didn't shrink from the pain of their stories, knowing the benefits of allowing them to speak about what happened to them. As I listened, the shield I had hidden behind came down. I'd found my tribe. It had taken years for Chad to get this far inside my walls. These women had done it in one night. I understood why Susan had spent time the first week creating a safe place for each of us, with clear ground rules.

The next week, I showed up with anticipation only to find the topic was anger. "If you don't get the anger out, it will make you sick," Susan said. "It increases your risk of heart disease, stroke, and your immune system won't function properly."

It made sense. I'd been tired and sick all winter. The abuse had brought up more anger than I knew how to deal with, and I hadn't wanted to cope with it. Good girls didn't get angry.

"Crashing your car or punching someone in the face leads to consequences you don't want, like going to jail." Susan smiled. "Tonight, we are going to go over healthy ways to release your anger. Anger isn't bad; it's just an emotion. Everyone feels anger. It's what we choose to do with it that's important."

Susan and I had talked extensively about anger. It raged inside me despite my insistence of maintaining a calm facade. I'd admitted my anger to a few in the hopes that accepting the fact it resided within me and was justified would allow it to dissipate. I allowed the tears to fall when the sadness overwhelmed me, but the anger was a fire ant to be stomped on. It resided in the dark room of shame within me, along with a sudden craving for alcohol. I'd gotten drunk a few times in my teens, but walked away from alcohol without a single regret. Now, I longed for a margherita or even a beer, and I never liked beer. Mormon's didn't drink alcohol. Good Mormons never even tasted it.

I thought of the disturbing craving while Susan talked about anger. I didn't know what it meant that I wanted alcohol. It could be rebellion or a need to dull the pain, but it seemed to be connected to the return of my memories. The fact that I wondered testified of the constant chipping away of my identity. I'd built a highly religious life that didn't mesh with alcohol. I worried that the process of remembering my abuse would destroy my life. My craving was another secret to add to the mountain weighing me down inside.

I snapped to attention when Susan picked up a small plastic bat with round holes in it. "I keep this plastic bat and a beanbag chair in my office. My only rule is that if you break the bat, you have to buy me a new one. That only happened once, and she bought me this cute bat with the holes, which I like better, so it worked out great."

She looked over the group. "Who wants to go first?"

Maggie volunteered. She always wore exercise clothes, coming straight from the gym because lifting weights kept her from killing herself.

She grabbed the bat and started slamming it into the beanbag. If anyone was going to break the bat, it would be Maggie. Soon she started mumbling words about her abusers with colorful language. Her savage attack continued until she lost her breath.

"Okay, I'm done," she said with a smile.

Another woman took a turn, and then another.

Refusing to get up in front of everyone, I begged off because I was sick again. After everyone who wanted to had taken a turn,

Susan pulled out a few phone books. She instructed us to write on the pages and then rip them out to release our anger. Not only did I rip them out of the book, I ripped the pages to shreds before putting them in the garbage.

"You can also go up into the mountains and throw raw eggs at the trees. It's very therapeutic, especially if you write names of your abusers on them."

It sounded fun, but I didn't dare go up into the mountains where I might get in trouble. Besides, it was still snowy up there.

After group ended, I chatted with Maggie about her weight-lifting, and she offered to teach me how to lift. We decided to meet that weekend.

On Saturday, I pulled up to a house with deep-gray bricks and a bright-red door. I knocked, and the door swung open to reveal a tall man with glasses and a long beard.

"Come in," he said.

"Thanks."

"I'm Maggie's husband. She's coming."

Maggie bounded in, muscles bulging against her tight clothes, blue gym bag slung over her shoulder. She got up on tiptoes while her husband leaned down and gave him a peck on the cheek.

He smiled. "Have fun."

"We will," Maggie said with a wicked gleam in her eye.

We drove to the gym in her car while we chatted about our families and lives, which helped me relax. I had a treadmill at home and had avoided the awkwardness of gyms, their complicated machines, and the confident, skinny people who frequented them.

Maggie taught me form as I lifted an embarrassingly light piece of white plastic pipe. When I passed inspection, she pulled out the lightest bar and put a tiny five-pound weight on each side.

"There is no way I can lift that."

"Sure you can."

Maggie corrected my form and instructed me to do ten reps while she lifted her own bar loaded with a rainbow of weights.

Despite struggling with my pathetic bar, I felt powerful. My body wasn't weak and sick anymore. I wanted to build my muscles to defend myself against any future attacks.

After the free weights, she moved me to the machines, working my arms, shoulders, and legs. Whenever I piped up that I couldn't do it, she'd talk me through it, and I accomplished what I believed my body couldn't. I was stronger than I thought.

Tired and hungry, we decided to get some nachos while we continued talking. Over chips and cheese, we found an easy friendship we both needed.

"I should go home, but I don't want to," Maggie said.

"My backyard isn't finished. Why don't we go throw eggs there? I bought five dozen a few days ago, so there are plenty to throw."

Maggie's smile widened. "Okay."

At my house, I pulled out two dozen eggs and grabbed some markers. We set to work drawing our abusers and pain. One egg boasted a man on fire, another a pervert, and some merely held the nasty words that lived inside us. Looking at the two dozen eggs spread before us, I pulled out a red marker and started jabbing them, leaving what looked like dark red stab wounds.

I grabbed an egg, turned to the tree, and let the egg fly. Satisfaction washed over me as it smashed into our tree. We took turns letting our anger explode into a gooey mess. I wasn't as good a shot as Maggie and managed to keep missing the tree, so I picked up the next egg, wrapped my fist around it, and squeezed it. My anger poured through my arm and into my hand until the egg exploded in my hand, sending yoke flying up in the air, higher than my head, as laughter burst from my throat. I was alive. My abusers did not control me; I was destroying them one by one.

Each week at group, I gained a greater understanding of how to deal with my situation in a safe environment, with other survivors. I experienced complete acceptance, which allowed me to lower the walls I'd maintained whenever I was around others.

By the end of our ten weeks together, I had forged bonds I didn't want to lose. I invited everyone over to my garage so they could also experience throwing eggs. We had snacks, threw darts at balloons with mean faces drawn on them, smashed eggs against a board using thin plastic sheeting for easy cleanup, and enjoyed our own secret club.

The lost friendships in my past faded as I created new friendships to take into my future.

16

FEARLESS

I emerged from hiding to attend a writer's conference, which I
enjoyed. The second day, I passed a few booths on my way to
my classes.

I don't trust people, especially those trying to sell me something, so there was no reason to stop and talk to Angie Fenimore,
owner of Calliope Writing Coach. I stopped anyway. We began
chatting, and I forgot there was anyone else around. There was
something about her that drew me in, an instant connection.
Angie was passionate about helping writers and promised me her
upcoming boutique conference would be life changing. I took her
card and left, knowing there wasn't money in the budget for it.

For the rest of the day and most of the next, I couldn't stop
thinking about Angie and a message I'd gotten from God. He
told me to stop finding reasons to pass by the opportunities he
put in my path. Only two weeks ago I'd faithfully promised to
accept any opportunities that came my way.

Though I didn't believe her conference would be life changing, I kept my promise to God and signed up anyway.

On a Friday morning in late June, I showed up at a small venue and picked a spot in the center of the U-shaped seats, where I could see the participants stretched around me and the presenters at the front.

The usual introductory information droned on, and then Angie began. Within minutes I was transfixed, my mind warring between giving my full attention to what she was saying and taking detailed notes so I wouldn't lose anything to my faulty memory.

It turned out she had a faulty memory as well. She remembered jumping off a high dive and sinking to the bottom of the pool, where she'd looked up to see her swim instructor blindly reaching for her. In reality, she had been lowered off the regular diving board to her swim instructor's outstretched arms. The incorrect memory had ruled her life for years—even though it had never happened.

"Belief is more powerful than fact," Angie said.

The first memory was belief; the second was what had actually happened. Her belief had overridden truth.

It was different for me. I'd believed I had a happy childhood, but I had, in fact, been abused. The abuse was more powerful than my belief or I wouldn't have suffered from chronic health problems, depression, and anxiety. Angie was wrong.

I'd spent my life trying to prove I was good enough, believing I was worthless and unlovable because of the abuse even though I couldn't remember what happened. My mind stuttered. I'd *believed* I was worthless and unlovable. Even though I'd thought I had a happy childhood, I believed the lies my abusers had told me, giving those lies more power than the facts. Angie was right.

"Write this down. These are the rules for writing," Angie said. "Number one, create your own reality; choose your own beliefs."

The words slammed into me. I needed to choose not to believe what my abusers had taught me and instead choose what I believed about myself and the world around me. I had given my abusers power over me by choosing to listen to the lies they told me about myself, but that was in the past. In the present and future, I could make different choices.

Angie continued talking as my mind absorbed this new concept. I struggled to listen with the insights buzzing around my head until she said, "Be afraid and do it anyway."

I'd spent years being afraid, but it had kept me safe. I had never broken a bone, gotten in an accident, or opened sketchy attachments to emails. But that safety had come at a price, which I finally understood after being in a wheelchair. I'd never traveled outside the United States, enjoyed parties, or learned how to feel alive.

I needed to change, right now, despite the fear. According to the doctors, my paralysis could come back at any time.

"Number two, operate with integrity." Angie looked at us. "What does it mean to operate with integrity? Honor your word. If you say you are going to do something, do it. If you don't do it, restore your integrity with that person."

I had no idea what this had to do with writing, but I knew I needed these rules in my life. I'd pretended to be a woman who honored her word, but all my broken promises to my kids paraded across my mind, testifying of the truth. My seemingly valid reasons were mere excuses.

After the first exhausting day of life-altering information, I staggered in the next day to see if the new information applied only to writing or to my current problems of overcoming abuse.

Our first guest presenter was Holly Stokes, otherwise known as the Brain Trainer.

"We are going to do a type of hypnosis, but you will be present and aware the entire time. This is how we work with the subconscious mind." She smiled. "Don't worry, this is not like the hypnosis shows you see, and I won't make you do weird things."

That was good because I refused to be hypnotized and hated hypnotist shows.

"Stand up and relax." Holly ran us through a few relaxation techniques and then said, "I want you to think of a color for confidence."

I pictured a beautiful, vibrant yellow.

"Now, I want you to think of a time when you experienced the feeling of confidence."

A host of thoughts and images passed before me. I settled on the image of myself standing tall, comfortable with myself and those around me. It wasn't a single event for me, more a feeling or state of being.

"Now, think of a color for accomplished."

Immediately, a vibrant hot pink came to mind.

"Think of a time when you experienced the feeling of being accomplished."

My mind went blank. I frantically searched for a memory. People had given me credit for adopting special-needs children, but it was God who'd told me to adopt. When they turned out to have problems, it wasn't because I chose it, it was because that's what they showed up with. I'd only struggled to survive the chaos.

I refocused, trying to pull up a memory. Getting married to a good guy the second time around? No, Chad had pushed, not me. Graduating high school? No, everyone did that. It was more a game of please the teacher than learning. Wait, I had returned to college to complete my associate's degree after dropping out for fourteen years. I'd taken one or two classes each semester with four young children to care for. I'd accomplished that. I held on to that image and allowed myself to relax as Holly moved on.

"Now, I want you to think of a color for comfort."

A soothing, clear blue entered my head.

"Think of a time when you felt comfortable."

I imagined lying in bed, snuggled up to my husband, the man who loved me unconditionally, the man I trusted and loved.

As we continued, Holly taught us how to access those feelings before we pitched our books to editors and agents.

I sat down in shock. Thirty years of adulthood and I believed I'd only accomplished one thing? I'd fought for my kids and all the interventions they needed. I'd participated in many hobbies I was good at. I'd helped others and was always busy . . . trying to prove I was good enough.

I'd started work only six months earlier, answering phones and doing paperwork. I lived a small, comfortable life. I hid from accolades to avoid expectations, new experiences to avoid humiliation, and people to avoid being hurt. It was all born of fear. I wasn't even sure what I was so afraid of, but Angie's words echoed in my head, "Be afraid and do it anyway."

The rest of the conference sped by with practical information I'd never gotten at any other writing conference I'd attended. I marveled at the learning I had almost walked right by.

At home a couple of days later, I pulled out a notebook and wrote "restore my integrity" across the top. Underneath, I wrote down all the broken promises I could remember. Items I'd borrowed and hadn't returned yet, commitments without firm deadlines to break through the procrastination. The list ran down the page. I approached each of my children to find out what else I hadn't completed. The list grew.

I committed to each child to honor my word and started immediately. I dropped things off to neighbors and took the kids to the local fun center where we had a great time riding go-karts and squirting each other in the bumper boats. My confidence grew.

I recommitted to God to do another thing Angie taught us: "When you meet opportunity, the answer is yes."

Her conference changed my life. I took control of my household and stopped letting the kids rule it with their tantrums. I embraced the fact that I wasn't a victim but a survivor. When the ladies in my AMAC shared a free retreat for women survivors of child sexual abuse, I signed up.

I took every opportunity to experience life. I enjoyed my son's graduation and tried new foods. I learned to set aside the pain and memories and enjoy life.

One day I mentioned fulfilling Chad's wish to ride the zipline at Olympic Park. Near where the ski jumpers competed in the 2002 Olympics, the park had set up a line that swooped down the mountain and hit speeds of up to fifty miles per hour.

We arrived at the park and hopped on the ski lift to take us to the zipline. At the top of the mountain we got in line, where I had plenty of time to watch people rush down the mountain, getting smaller until they were no larger than ants. I forced my eyes away and gazed across the valley at the mountains as a distraction.

"The view is beautiful from up here," I said.

"Yeah." Chad wrapped one arm around me. I wasn't sure if it was to calm my nerves or because he was excited.

The line for single riders was much shorter than the line for two parallel riders, so we opted for the single line.

"You want to go first?" Chad asked.

"No, you can go first." My fear of heights spoke up.

"Okay."

Chad geared up and calmly flew down the mountain. When he made it safely to the bottom, my brain assured me I would make it too, but the rest of my body didn't get the memo.

Suddenly I had to face my fears alone. The workers hooked me securely into my harness and put me into position, leaning me against the solid green metal gate. I refused to look like an idiot in front of the long line behind me, so I stayed in position and listened to my heart pound, feeling like a horse waiting for the starting gun.

The gate swung open, and I was on my way down. The smooth motion gave no hint of the speed. My adrenaline faded to the anticlimactic lull at the bottom. I came to conquer my fears, but in the end, there was nothing to be afraid of. I craved something more adventuresome.

Chad and I hiked to the smallest K40 ski jump to go extreme tubing. Instead of the icy snow I'd seen during the Olympics, the jump was covered in synthetic green thatching. To help the tubes slide, large sprinklers switched on from time to time to keep the surface slick. A worker told us to grab helmets and tubes. Looking down the steep slope was completely different from looking up from the bottom.

"You have to go first to show me I won't die," I said as I snapped the helmet strap under my chin.

Chad laughed.

"I don't know why I'm doing this. There is reason for fear, you know, to keep us from doing dumb things that might get us killed."

"You can do it. I know you can."

Chad went first, and I listened to his exultant whoop.

As I gingerly stepped out on the surface, the guide said, "Be careful. The surface can be slippery." I sat in the middle of a large black tube with nothing except a helmet to protect me.

"Stay seated the entire time," the guide said as he gave me a shove.

I wanted out, but it was too late. The tube plunged downward at a slope only slightly better than a freefall. A scream tore from my throat and didn't end until I got to the bottom.

I did it!

"That was so much fun!" I yelled to Chad while I was still twenty feet away.

"See, I knew you'd like it. Ready for the K90?" To ride the longer jump, participants were required to complete the K40.

"No way! I'll watch you do it."

One of the guides turned to me. "If you can do this one, you can do the K90. It isn't any steeper, just longer."

I looked over at the height of the longest jump.

"I'll go up with you and decide there," I said to Chad, though I had no intention of going down the monster.

We left our tubes for the truck to haul back up and got in line at the ski lift. Riding up was my favorite part. It gave me a bird's-eye view of the mountainside with its boulders, bushes, and towering pines.

"If I go down the K90, you have to buy me that gold medal in the gift shop," I said.

"If you go down the K90, you will have earned that medal. I'll buy it if you do it."

"Promise?"

We got off the lift and hiked down to the start of the jump. I wanted the gold medal, and I wanted to be with Chad. I was afraid, but I put on a helmet anyway, telling myself I had the option to change my mind whenever I wanted to. Chad went first, disappearing over the crest. It took a long time for him to come into view and roll to a stop before he jumped up, turned around, and waved.

I inched my way out to the designated spot and looked over the edge to see that it went down, down, down. *This is crazy.*

Be afraid and do it anyway. I envisioned the shiny gold medal around my neck and sat down. The guide pushed, and my screaming began. I screamed until the air ran out, gulped in, and screamed louder than I ever had in my life.

Fifty miles an hour on the zipline felt leisurely; hitting close to fifty on a tube felt like going ninety without brakes. I skidded farther than Chad had by quite a distance and stopped close to where he now stood.

"How was it?"

"Terrifying!" I shouted with wide eyes. "I need to go again!"

Chad laughed, and we trekked up the mountain again. I reveled in the adrenaline that made my body feel invincible.

After our second ride, I said, "Let's go on the bobsled run."

"Really?"

"Sure. We're here. Not many people in the world get to ride in a bobsled."

"Okay." Chad's face lit up with the excitement.

We bought our tickets, signed disclosures that we were aware of the danger, and hopped a ride on a shuttle to the top of the bobsled run. On the way, we learned that this run was the second fastest in the world, the fastest to allow nonathletes to ride, and one of only two in the world that let nonathletes ride from the top. The bus was filled with vacationers from around the world taking the opportunity to careen down the bobsled run with a professional driver.

The warnings at the top almost dissuaded me. This was a ride that posed a serious risk of death, but if I backed out, I'd lose my money and have to take the walk of shame down the mountain in front of a world audience. I knew the ride had to be fairly safe or they wouldn't allow nonathletes to ride. I stayed quiet and put on my helmet.

"Keep your back completely straight, look ahead, and hold your arms out against the sides of the sled. It's very important to keep that form during the whole ride."

Chad helped push the bobsled in front of us, and then it was our turn. We climbed into the stationary sled equipped with wheels rather than runners. I got in right behind the driver, and Chad slid in behind me. It was too late to change my mind now.

We flew down the track like ants in a bullet—a bullet flying through gravel. I struggled to hold my position against the vibrations of the huge sled.

First turn. *I'm doing good.*

Hold your back straight and look ahead. I focused on the black wavy lines on the back of the driver's helmet. The second turn tugged at my body, but I kept my position, hating everything about the experience.

The third turn pulled my head to the side and out of form. *Don't hit his helmet, or he'll know you broke position!*

I'd barely recovered when we hit turn four and my body wasn't strong enough to counteract the pull of a 4-G, almost 360-degree turn. The force pulled my body down, hunching my shoulders and yanking my head to the side while my helmet shook violently. My puny arms were useless.

Will my head hit the side of the sled? Will it hit the driver? I hate this! Why am I here?

The turn finally straightened out, and I was able to slowly return to my position. Everything hurt—my legs pressed against Chad's shoes, my back, my neck. My arms hitting against the metal sides of the sled was the worst.

The rest of the run blurred together in a running commentary in my head to distract me from the punishment being inflicted on my body.

It only lasts a minute. It will be over soon.

My muscles can't do this. I want out!

How many more turns can there be?

I hate this.

This must be the last turn.

Another? No!

I'm going to die.

At last, the sled slowed down. Even at half the speed of a normal bobsled run, we'd made it in just over a minute. I had a new respect for Olympians who made it look easy and smooth.

I climbed out of the sled, thanked the driver with a smile, and walked out and around the building.

"That was amazing," Chad said. "What did you think?"

I carefully turned my aching head to make sure I was far enough away no one would hear me. "It was horrible! I am never, ever doing anything like that again. I deserve the big medal now!" Chad laughed. "Really, it was the worst minute of my life. My brains felt like Jell-O in an earthquake."

"But you did it. You even surprised me."

"I should have let you go by yourself."

"I wouldn't have gone without you." Chad reached out and held my hand.

"Well, I'm never going again."

Chad chuckled again at my passionate outbursts. "Okay."

Every step testified of the beating the sled had given my body. Muscles ached and bruises throbbed, while a tendon in my shoulder testified of having been pulled too far. And yet, despite the aches, something new washed over me: a sense of fearlessness.

So what if I hated it? I'd survived. For the rest of my life, I could boast that I'd ridden in a bobsled down an Olympic track. I'd come to conquer my fear on the zipline but ended up discovering that extreme tubing down Olympic Nordic tracks was amazing and that I was bold enough to go down the scariest ride I could imagine. I'd spent years hanging back, watching others and never participating. Now I was the one daring to face death, with an incredible story to share. It was worth the bumps and bruises to realize I was fearless.

17

FAILURE

My journey of discovery and healing had resulted in broken promises and an emotionally distant Mom for my kids. I'd read that trauma was coded into the DNA and passed on to the children. It made me sick to think that any of what happened to me had caused them pain, but I knew it did.

The internal change began to show in external ways when I decided I needed to step up and be a better parent. The prenatal drug-and-alcohol exposure Amber and Gavin experienced had caused brain damage that affected their physical and mental health. While other parts of the brain can be reprogrammed to compensate, it takes work and time. I'd already put years into helping them, yet still they struggled.

I always did my best, fighting for treatments for my kids, but Gavin and Amber pushed me past what I knew how to deal with. They had both been at day treatment centers, seen specialists, had surgeries, and been given huge chunks of my time to the exclusion of the other kids. I needed to create a better home environment for everyone. When I began establishing rules that needed to be followed, Gavin and Amber pushed back.

And while trying to cope with a situation that only seemed to be getting worse, I had more flashbacks, helping me see that physical abuse was just as much a part of what had happened to me as the sexual abuse.

#flashback
Strong arms grabbed me from behind, twisting my arm across my back. Hot breath tickled my skin as threats were whispered into my ear.

#flashback
Pain exploded from the back of my head as a faceless person yanked a handful of my hair to control me.

I didn't understand the significance of the second flashback for days. One of the first things I did after moving to Salt Lake City was experiment with shorter hairstyles until I finally settled on a pixie cut. In all the years since, I rarely grew my hair out, and when I did, I cut it off again, keeping the hair around my ears and neck short. It had become my trademark. Mom and I said we were short-hair girls and we wore the style well.

My hair hadn't remained short because I wanted it that way; it was another reaction to abuse. I refused to let anyone control me that way again, so I had cut it off. Another piece off my identity had slipped away.

I thought that because I'd smiled in the psych ward, it proved I was better adjusted. I began thinking it made more sense to be the one crying in the psych ward rather than the one smiling. I hadn't smiled because I was happy; it was my way of coping, my way of pretending. I wondered if my whole identity were an act. If I dropped the act, who would I be? There were no answers.

At home, things got worse. Amber kicked a hole in the wall when I took away her technology for a day as a consequence for her hurting Gavin. Gavin lunged at me with a knife because I told him he couldn't have candy. And while Amber eventually came around, Gavin became dangerous.

#trigger

"Gavin, you need to go upstairs to calm down," I said.

He swore at me, knowing how much swear words bothered me, but I remained calm. "Gavin, you need to go upstairs to calm down."

I reached out for his arm to guide him upstairs, but he twisted, flinging out his arm and hitting me in the stomach. I remembered another time I'd been hit in the stomach, and my fear exploded as our arms got tangled and he shoved me against the wall with his body.

I'm not going to let you hurt me!

I was trapped between the present and the past. Gavin wasn't my child; he was an abuser, and I'd promised never to let him hurt me again.

The rage intensified, giving me added strength to get control of my "monster" and wrestle him to the ground. I needed to hurt him, to show him I wasn't weak and helpless anymore.

Thankfully, the present intruded, and I realized it was Gavin. I held on to that bit of truth with every bit of mental strength I had, but he kept kicking and fighting to get free. If he didn't stop, he'd overpower me, and I'd tip fully into my flashback.

"Stop it, or I'll hurt you!" The sound of my voice in my ears was wrong; it wasn't me, I slipped back into my crazed thoughts. "Stop! I'm going to hurt you if you don't stop it!" I pushed against him, trying to control his flailing, when I looked into his terror-filled eyes. I jumped away as if burned. He was scared of me, his mother. What had I become? He wasn't one of my abusers; he was a little boy lost in mental illness, just like me.

I noticed Amber sitting at the computer several feet away, her eyes wide in fear. Chad was halfway down the stairs, running toward the noise we'd made.

I couldn't face them. I ran past Chad to my bedroom and curled into a fetal position, ashamed and shaking. I knew Chad was with the kids, taking care of everything. I wanted to be a better person, not a worse one. I wanted to stand up for myself, not scare anyone.

My grip on reality was thin some days. I hated who I was becoming, yet what could I do? I needed to keep myself and my kids safe, but Gavin was strong enough to have kicked in the front door even with the dead bolt locked and put a three-foot crack down the brand-new doorframe. I was in a no-win situation, and fear ruled far too often.

Chad came in and gently laid his hand on my back. "Are you okay? What can I do for you?" His voice was soft and loving.

I had to get away from this man who was so good to me. I didn't deserve him. I had to get away from the kids, who needed a better mother. I got up, grabbed my keys, and drove to Maggie's house. She was the only one who could understand. I parked in her driveway, and we talked in my van.

She'd had a rough week battling suicidal ideation. We talked for hours about our struggles and shame. Around 1:00 a.m. I knew I needed to go home and fix the problems I'd caused. My family needed help.

The kids went to school the next day, and I avoided thinking about what had happened. Amber had talked to the school counselor, who was probably the one that called the Department of Child and Family Services. A woman talked to Gavin at school and stopped by the house when I was out running errands.

It seemed crazy. No one had fought or done more for their kids than I had. I was a normal, suburban mom living in a nice neighborhood who made sure her kids were so kind that the older three were constantly being bullied at school.

But I was also emotionally exhausted. I decided if Child Services thought they could find a better mom for my kids, they were welcome to give me a break.

As it turned out, in talking to Gavin, who openly admitted to hurting and threatening others, the social worker was more concerned about my safety and the safety of my family than me hurting Gavin. I hoped they could help me, but they were only there to investigate.

I talked to Gavin's therapist about everything that had happened and how Nicole had nightmares about Gavin stabbing her in her sleep. I needed to know how to keep everyone safe.

We took anything that could be used as a weapon out of Gavin's room and installed a lock so we could keep him in his room when he was dangerous. She insisted that whenever Gavin was violent, we needed to call the police to teach him his behavior was unacceptable.

Locking his room helped, but I had to be able to get Gavin into the room first. He put holes in the Sheetrock and dents in the solid wood door but didn't hurt himself or others. Weeks passed, and we did the best we could while I continued therapy and tried to cope not only with the abuse but feeling like I had an abuser I couldn't control, or escape from, in my own house.

The next time he got out of control, I videotaped portions of it with my phone so others could see for themselves how my adorable, charming eight-year-old son transformed into a rage-filled child who didn't resemble Gavin at all. Gavin screamed at me to stop recording. He escaped his dad's grasp and lunged at me, attacking me until Chad got him under control again. At this point, Chad was working from home or using vacation days to keep us safe, because he was the only one strong enough to hold Gavin and keep him from hurting himself or others. We did as the therapist instructed and called the police.

The call instantly sobered Gavin. "Are they taking me to jail?" he asked.

"No. They are just going to make sure we are all safe," I responded.

By the time the police arrived, Gavin was calm, anxious about what they might do.

"What is it you want us to do?" an officer asked.

"We need to take him to the hospital again, but he has gotten more violent in the car, which isn't safe. Last time I stopped the car, he opened the door and started running down the road. We need you to take him to Primary Children's so he can be admitted." This would be Gavin's third hospital stay in the last few months.

"We can't take him in our squad car, but we can call an ambulance if you really think you need one."

At the talk of returning to the hospital, Gavin began yelling, swearing, and hitting me. One officer called the ambulance, Chad worked to get Gavin under control, and the other officer and I discussed the situation until the ambulance arrived.

To Gavin, a ride in the ambulance was a treat, so he eagerly climbed in while we followed in the van.

At the hospital, Gavin was calm and charming. While the nurses looked after him, we talked to the social worker about getting him admitted in a separate room.

"When you tell Gavin he's going to be admitted, you need to have security guards waiting. Last time we were here and told him, security had to be called," I said.

The social worker looked at his chart. "Okay."

"I won't be able to be there either. He attacks me."

"I'll get everything started, and then I'll come back so we can tell him when we have everything in place."

We chatted with Gavin until the social worker came into the room. I saw two security guards waiting outside.

As soon as she told him he was going to the hospital, he lunged for the door, kicking, swearing, and doing everything he could to get away.

It took a large security guard and Chad to hold him, while another guarded the door to make sure he didn't get out. Gavin kicked, writhed, and tried head-butting Chad until the security guard decided that someone was going to get hurt if they didn't sedate him. All I could do was wait helplessly outside the room, listening in and occasionally peeking through the window. Both burly security guards held my screaming boy down so the nurse could give him the shot, which finally calmed him down, causing him to break into sobs. He hated being out of control as much as we did.

The hospital staff recommended that Gavin be sent to the Utah State Hospital, a residential treatment center for kids who struggled with extreme violence. Our only other choice was a failed adoption in order to protect the other kids.

The expected three-to-four-month wait was reduced to three weeks due to the severity of the situation. I breathed a sigh of relief, knowing I wouldn't have to go through every day terrified of getting hurt, him hurting someone else, or someday being the mother of a kid who shot up a school.

Chad dropped Calvin off at college while I stayed home with Gavin. Calvin didn't mind, he was used to me missing milestones in his life, but it saddened me.

It was difficult to drop Gavin off at the hospital, but it was also a major relief. I needed to use my time to heal, work through the abuse, and be ready to be a better mother when he got released. Once a week, Chad and I drove the hour and a half to the hospital, where we had family therapy and got a chance to see Gavin, even if for only five minutes.

The change helped everyone. The constant tension and yelling in the house disappeared. I worked through my issues and to repair the damage that had been done by me being in the wheelchair and Gavin's threats.

The kids still at home began coming out of their rooms and participating in home life again. Gavin struggled, but he was getting the help he needed, and we started seeing great improvements. The staff at the hospital and his school there were amazing.

Chad and I even had the opportunity to return to Oregon to the bed-and-breakfast on the coast we had loved so much, knowing Gavin was taken care of.

I began to believe I had a chance at living a normal life if I could get through the rest of my healing.

18

STRENGTH

We visited Gavin the day before Thanksgiving and then traveled out of town for my family's biannual gathering. With the progress I had made, I was comfortable being myself and was actually able to have fun. There were some odd vibes, like no one knew how to act around me, and some odd questions, but I shrugged them off, being used to changes in the way people interacted with me now that I'd discovered abuse in my past.

My turn to attend the retreat for victims of childhood sexual abuse arrived shortly after Thanksgiving. I worried someone else needed it more than I did, but the organizer shrugged that off and told me when to arrive.

As I drove the hour to our meet-up point, my nervousness increased. I had basic details of our activities but no control over where I would sleep, what I would eat, or what I would be doing. I almost turned around and drove home. Then Angie's words echoed in my head. "Be afraid and do it anyway." I turned the music up and began to sing along.

I arrived at our meeting spot, a restaurant just off the freeway, and made awkward small talk with the other participants. The coordinators arrived and asked us to follow their cars to where the retreat was located. The lead car headed out, and we snaked our way up into the mountains. We pulled into the drive of a huge mansion, where some women were directed into the front entry and others, like me, waited to be shown to the cabin. I was disappointed to be staying in a cabin instead of the beautiful main house until a woman led us to a huge log structure nestled in the pines. They had a completely different concept of what constituted a cabin.

On the bed in my room lay several gifts: personal notes of encouragement from strangers, a cozy blanket, a journal, a folder that held my schedule, and a book about abuse. The twenty or so women attending were broken into smaller groups, with group leaders for the day and someone who would stay all night in case we needed anything. Every detail, down to the outside night guard, had been thoughtfully placed to help us feel safe.

Our first activity was to create kintsugi bowls, something I was excited to do. An assortment of bowls sat in the middle of the table, each one unique. I snatched up a gorgeous white bowl with blue flowers painted on the sides.

The first thing we were asked to do was to place a towel over our bowl and break it with a special hammer. My roommate cried, not wanting to break something whole and beautiful. She wanted someone else to do it for her, but eventually she grabbed the hammer, breaking her bowl on the first try. We all cheered for her, understanding it wasn't about breaking the bowl.

My bowl was thick and strong and didn't break the first time I hit it. I swung again and, still, it remained whole. I put more force behind it and heard an interesting sound. I lifted the towel resting over the bowl and was disappointed to see three neat pieces.

I passed along the hammer and stared at the three pieces. My bowl didn't represent how broken I was inside. When everyone else finished, I asked if I could break mine again. I hit one of the pieces, and it broke in two. Still unsatisfied, I hit another piece that broke into four. I now had seven pieces, matching the seven abusers I'd uncovered.

Now it was time to rebuild. Using a Popsicle stick, I smeared a mixture of gold powder and epoxy onto a broken piece of bowl and pressed it into the round base that had remained unbroken. I checked and double-checked that I had everything lined up perfectly as the pressure of holding the pieces together made them slide apart.

When one piece dried enough to stay, I began another. I pressed it against the first two pieces for a moment before moving on. As I set the next piece in place, I realized I'd let the last piece go too quickly and it had slid down. I hurried to hold it in place, worried about the new piece drying before I could get everything put together.

Holding the pieces, I understood the metaphor. Putting my broken self together would take time. If I rushed, I'd have to go back. I also wanted it to be perfect, as if it had never broken in the first place.

Holding more than one piece caused the alignment to be slightly off. My bowl wasn't perfect but I had accomplished what I set out to do—make the bowl whole and complete so it could hold water and be of use.

It was an emotional task that manifested in diverse ways. Some bowls had little holes to let in light, and some looked a little wonky, but the differences only made each bowl more unique and beautiful. It took work and patience to take a broken bowl and create something new, beautiful, and strong in its place.

We ate dinner at the mansion and then attended a class where I learned about the brain science surrounding trauma.

A new day brought new experiences. We attended group off-site so that the memories we were going to talk about wouldn't be attached to our relaxation at the retreat. I listened to others and then spilled out my story about the empty Christmas present Kyle had given me and how I still saw the inside of that empty box, heard the cruel laughter, and felt worthless. I received love and support from the women and gave it to them in turn as they shared pieces of their stories. We felt worthless, broken, and filled with shame. We had all struggled to trust, love, and experience normal intimacy.

In hearing their stories and the guilt and shame they expressed about the grooming process, I was able to clearly see how these women were not at fault and how my own feelings of shame and guilt over these aspects of the abuse were incorrect. A new power flooded me.

My abusers were skilled at the grooming process, training me to return for more abuse. I'd spent my life blaming my teenage self for throwing her life away. But it wasn't her fault. It wasn't my fault. It was a normal reaction to the abuse I had hidden away in my mind.

I had blamed my parents for not loving me and held on to the few things that confirmed that belief rather than accepting the countless instances where their love shone through.

My mother knew something was wrong during those teenage years and had sought out that highly recommended child psychiatrist whom I'd faithfully gone to for six months until he'd told Mom he had done all he could because there was something I wasn't ready to talk about. I left and got engaged to Carson within weeks. I'd blamed everything that had happened in that relationship on my psychiatrist giving up on me when I obviously needed help.

My eyes were being opened. If that therapist had managed to break through to the abuse at the time, I would have committed suicide. I didn't have the coping skills I developed over the years. I remembered working hard, leaving in a cold sweat every session. He had helped me gain a sense of worth and become strong enough to get myself out of that abusive relationship. I'd been blaming the wrong people. It wasn't my fault or theirs; we had done the best we could and managed to survive. It was my abusers who were to blame.

The next day I was able to pound out my anger in Muay Thai, a form of kickboxing that is therapeutic for abuse survivors. I focused all my pent-up emotions on my targets and felt empowered rather than tired.

That night in a drum circle, we each found our own rhythms, which were woven together to create a unique song that thrummed through my bones. I'd found my people, my tribe, in a place of understanding and love.

They even treated us to a photoshoot, with stylists who did our hair and makeup. When it was my turn, I said, "I've never found a way to look both feminine and strong with my short hair."

I let them do whatever they wanted, and when I turned around and looked in the mirror, I was astonished at the woman staring back at me. She was feminine and strong as well as incredibly beautiful.

All of this was given to me without expectation or price. I had to make my way to the retreat in Utah, but once there, everything was covered, from the donated journals to the gourmet food prepared by a chef.

Never had I realized the love and value others placed on me as a person. They did not help me because I did something for them first. They didn't make me prove I deserved to be there. They merely offered help and healing.

On the drive to our second group session, while the other ladies listened in, I talked with one of the ladies in my group about my experiences with Angie and the coaching I'd received from her.

"We were struggling with staying positive, and Angie told us to get a small box and fill it with positive sayings so we'd have something to turn to when we struggled. Then she and her husband sent handwritten notes to each of us," I said. "I don't have a box yet, but I realized how powerful it is to send an actual letter. No one seems to do that anymore."

The woman next to me put her hand on my arm and looked at me. "That's your answer."

I looked at her in confusion.

"That's what you need to do to get rid of the empty box from Christmas. Fill a cardboard box with all the good things you have in your life, and then it won't be empty anymore."

I thought about her idea for a moment. "It's almost Christmas again. Maybe I can gather messages until Christmas, then take them out and burn the box."

Other women chimed in, excited about the idea. While their chatting turned to other things, my mind remained on the possibilities for healing the emptiness inside.

I agreed to drop off three of the women at the airport so we could get tattoos and enjoy a bit more time together Mai and Rachelle were from Canada and Danielle lived in California. We climbed in my van and drove to Salt Lake City to a tattoo parlor my friend Maggie recommended.

Mai and I had never gotten a tattoo before. She wanted a tattoo of a kintsugi bowl, showing that her broken places were now made strong. I had been planning my tattoo for about eight months already, but my drawings were at home.

Danielle pulled up a picture of the large arm tattoo she wanted, while Rachelle pondered over the flock of birds she wanted to fly across her wrist.

Only two people were allowed back at a time, so Mai and Danielle went first, while I explained to a tattoo artist what I wanted. I immediately liked his rendition despite it not being exactly what I had envisioned.

Danielle and Mai returned and then crossed the street for a beer. It was my turn. My new friend sat next to me to hold my hand through the pain.

I wondered if I would eventually regret it but figured if I'd wanted a tattoo for thirty years, it wasn't likely to change. I'd spent eight months pondering what I wanted and where I wanted it, using fake tattoos in various spots to try them out.

I talked to Rachelle, gripped her hand, and eventually the tattoo artist was finished. I gazed down at my left front bicep and at the black ink now permanently etched into my skin. It was on the left to signify it was something close to my heart and on my muscle to remind me of the strength I possessed. Perched on a single, rounded flame was a butterfly shaped almost like a heart. The butterfly signified my transformation, my new life, and my power to fly.

I'd spend years hating hearts, and so the shape was intentional, a reminder that I needed to accept my inner child: The little girl who dotted her i's with a heart in an attempt to be cool. The girl who loved pale pink and ballerinas. The child my abusers silenced and destroyed.

The flame represented the refining fire I had been through. Fire could destroy, or it could transform. I chose transformation. The burning could hurt, but in the end, it produced something purer and stronger than before.

My friends and I had dinner before I dropped them off at the airport. It was sad to see them go, knowing I wasn't likely to see them again, but I carried the strength they gave me inside, with a tattoo that would help me remember them always.

I had to call Mom to share the many breakthroughs I'd experienced during the retreat, as well as the power getting a tattoo represented for me. Not only had I reclaimed my body, I had reclaimed parts of myself I'd rejected.

"Mom, Marie kept trying to get me to stand up for myself and telling me I was spineless, but it isn't true."

"No, it's not."

"God told me if I stayed with Carson, I would be destroyed, so I left. Even though it was God who saved me, I still had to do it."

"God may have helped you, but that wasn't why you left."

"What do you mean?"

"You planned it for months. I remember you calling me when you were still in California. You told me you were going to leave him but you needed to make sure he lived close to his mother and had an apartment and job so he would be okay after you left. You were the one who convinced him to move to Utah so you could leave."

"Really?"

"Yes. I was scared you wouldn't be able to do it, but you did. You orchestrated the whole thing."

"All these years I've told people that the reason I was able to escape was because you prayed for me every day and God told me to leave."

"I prayed, and God helped, but you are the one who did it."

"That doesn't sound spineless to me. That sounds strong."

"You have never been spineless; I've been amazed at your strength."

"I love you, Mom."

"I love you too."

I hung up the phone, warmed not only by the words we had shared but by the unspoken love that was rare for my family.

I'd carried the words of my sister—that I was spineless—everywhere, but I ejected them from my heart. I had chosen to leave Carson, knowing the relationship was bad at least six months before I'd actually left. I had seen through his lies and promises to change long before he told me he'd been unfaithful. I'd done everything I could to make things work, and when it hadn't, I convinced him to move back to Utah, making him think it was his idea.

Despite the emotional, physical, and sexual abuse, I'd reacted with kindness, making sure he had a support system in place. I'd had offers from my best friend and Mom to come down and get me, but I'd wanted to make sure he wouldn't be left alone, far from his family. I needed to leave with a clear conscience, and I had.

I rebuilt my life. If I had done it then, I could certainly do it again. My abusers had taught me to submit or get hurt, then to blame myself. They'd taught me to hate myself, but they were wrong, and deep down I had always known it. I'd battled their lies. They had taught me I needed to earn love, but God taught me I was worthy of love, even when I sinned.

I thought of the girls of eleven and twelve I'd interacted with, even my own children. I would never blame a child for abuse.

In that moment, I stopped blaming myself.

I needed to fill my empty box.

19

GOING UP IN SMOKE

I stared into the empty cardboard box I'd found in the garage, transported back to that moment—my shoulders hunched, the mocking laughter in my ears, the shame and worthlessness paralyzing me. I cleared these images from my mind and deposited the box in my office.

That box and the associated memories taunted me whenever I was in the room and haunted me when I fled. For days the power the box held over me prevented me from putting anything in it. I pretended to ignore it and checked my email instead. A message from my youngest brother caught my eye, and I eagerly opened it. Instead of being supportive, his words were accusatory.

From the outside looking in, this looks a lot like a little older boy giving a younger girl attention and a girl who liked the attention and was willing to do things she knew she shouldn't get that attention. Now, like I said, I am telling you from a perspective, not knowing what really happened. I just know that if you kept going back when you clearly knew better (this is an assumption being that I knew better and I grew up in the same house, so I assume you knew better) and seemed to be wanting to play more, maybe you were more willing than you let on.

If the email had stopped there, I could chalk it up to misunderstanding, but he continued to judge every aspect of my life, including how I'd chosen to raise my kids, my struggles with religion, my asking for prayers, and even where I'd chosen to live. He claimed I was spending my time with a "woe is me" attitude despite what looked like a pretty great life. I reread the end of his lengthy email.

You have chosen to be a victim because it is easy and because people will tell you how terrible life is and how strong you are. Then the tip of the iceberg was that wonderful tattoo you got. It screams give me attention, treat me like a victim. I choose not to be a victim in my life and thought that we were taught to take responsibility for our actions and stand up and move on. I know you will not think so when you read this, but I say these things because I love you.

It was like opening a package that turned out to be a bomb, only instead of scarring me on the outside, the words were a knife that filleted my heart. He stated others in the family felt the same way, but he was the only one willing to speak up in order to help me. I lost what little connection I had to my family that day. I was truly alone.

I had no interest in celebrating my favorite holiday of the year. I loved Christmas, but I was usually sick. Instead of a virus or infection this year, it was a soul sickness. The empty box I held inside grew, and I knew nothing could fill it.

My brother knew almost nothing of what had happened to me. I sent him a couple of sentences about being raped in the barn. He immediately apologized, but the damage had been done.

I reached out in a desperate attempt to stop my slide into the abyss of my thoughts. I posted a brief explanation of the Christmas party and the empty gift on Facebook and asked my friends to share positive messages to put in my box. I decided that on Christmas Day, I would take the messages out and burn the box.

Chad saw my post and wanted to help. "I want to make you a hardwood box to put the messages in. Would that be okay?"

"That would be amazing."

Over the next week, old and new friends on Facebook responded by sending memes and notes. I heard from people I barely knew telling me how my words and example positively impacted them. I printed each meme and message and mounted them on colored cardstock.

I don't know if family members didn't see the post or didn't know what to say, but I got no messages from any extended family, only my husband. The bonds of blood dissolved, and a new family of friends who knew and loved me was created.

Hope resurged and gave me strength to face the Christmas season. Strength was a double edged sword. It made the carrying of my burdens easier so I could deal with adding another stone onto the pile. I didn't do it consciously, but my subconscious took note. A few brief flashbacks stole the little bit of peace I'd managed. It was easier to deal with the memory than try to run and hide from it so I allowed the rest of the memory of that fateful Christmas party to surface.

#memory

I sat in Kyle's room, the empty box on my lap. Skinny's arm was extended, the quarter held between his finger and thumb. I took the metal disc and held it in my palm as he turned and left as well.

I put the box on the floor and picked up my jeans. I slid the quarter into the pocket and got dressed. The quarter confused me.

Bandit burst into the room by himself and shut the door. "That might be enough for those boys, but I'm a man. Take off your clothes."

I barely shook my head no, staring at him in fear.

He grabbed a fistful of hair at the back of my head and yanked hard. He leaned into my face and snarled, "I told you to take them off. You are going to do what I say and be quiet, or I swear I'll kill you, capeesh?"

He released me, and I did as he asked.

"On the floor," he commanded.

I lay down, my legs together to the side. With his own pants down now, he pushed between me and raped me quick and rough.

He stood up, then zipped and buttoned his jeans. "Don't tell anyone, not even Kyle. If you do, I'll come back and kill you in your sleep right after I rape you again."

Fear blossomed, and I dared not say anything. He left and bounded down the stairs.

"Found it," I heard him say.

I sat up, knowing I needed to get away. I pulled on my underwear and then my pants. With my hands still on the zipper, Kyle returned.

"That was fun. You did good."

I stared at him, the betrayal, hurt, and pain radiating from me.

His mood shifted, his eyes becoming hard. "It's your own fault. All I wanted was a little pussy. Next time you won't lay there like a frigid bitch."

I stayed frozen, seeing not a boyfriend but someone who hated me.

"Now that you're all warmed up, let's finish what we started."

He undid his pants and pulled them off. My brain shut down. He reached forward and unzipped my pants before pushing his hand inside.

"I can tell you had fun too." He slid his finger inside me. "See, that's proof. If you didn't like it, you wouldn't be wet."

He slid my pants and underwear down. "Come on." He nodded to the bed.

I didn't move.

"I know you had fun. I was standing there the whole time. Don't be upset. I didn't have time to get you something, okay?"

He peered into my eyes and flexed his jaw. "Just get on the bed."

I turned to the bed, my pants down at my knees, planning on sitting down to take my pants off.

Kyle grabbed me from behind, his arm pressing into my abdomen, making it hard to breathe. He leaned into me, his lips by my ear. "Don't you dare tell anyone about today."

I remained still while he squeezed harder. Terror rendered me mute.

"I mean it. If you ever tell anyone, I'll send Bandit to your house. He's not as nice as I am."

I'll kill you in your sleep. The earlier threat from Bandit echoed in my head.

I complied, lying on the bed with my legs out now that I knew what I was supposed to do.

"That's my girl."

He climbed on and raped me more gently than Bandit, but it still hurt. When he finished, he got dressed and picked up my underwear off the floor. "I'll give you five dollars for this pair."

"Okay." What else was there to say?

He wiped the underwear across my pain and put it in his drawer before handing me five dollars. He left to check on his siblings, whom he was babysitting, so I put the money in my pocket with the quarter. I got dressed, crept out of the house, and walked home, my jeans rubbing uncomfortably. I never said anything to anyone.

No wonder Christmas had always been such a difficult time of year for me. I pushed down my feelings and pretended to enjoy the season for the sake of the kids.

Chad presented me with a beautiful mahogany box inlaid with maple accents.

"I love it. It's beautiful." I ran my finger along the smooth edge, noticing how every place the wood met was joined perfectly. I hugged him, then picked up the box and held it to my chest. I walked to the living room and set it under the Christmas tree.

On my way back, I glanced at the cardboard box I'd moved into my bedroom. I stopped to look at the small collection of pictures and words inside. There weren't many, but they were powerful.

The next couple of weeks brought only one or two new messages. The scarcity made the messages I received more meaningful. I planned to read the messages again on Christmas Eve before transferring them to my wooden box.

Christmas Eve came and went. My eight-year-old spent Christmas night in the hospital. It broke my heart not to have him home for Christmas morning, and I was in no mood to burn my cardboard box.

Christmas Day was almost over when my husband set the wooden box next to me on the bed.

"I know you're avoiding it. Do you want some help?"

I sighed. "Yes."

He retrieved the cardboard box, set it down as well, and joined me to offer support.

I lifted the lid of my new box to find a message my husband had written and sealed with his wax seal. I slipped my finger under the paper to break the seal. There weren't many words, but I knew they were from his heart.

"I love you," I said to him.

I returned his note to the box and pulled a message from the cardboard box. I read it and placed it in the wooden box. Healing washed over me as I repeated this with each message.

I carried the empty box out to the garage, where Chad lit a fire in a small can stove. I placed the cardboard box faceup on the center. I wanted to see the emptiness filled with fire.

Smoke crept along the edges and seeped through the bottom flaps. The scent reminded me of the campfires we'd enjoyed with our kids. Eventually, a round hole appeared, black and burning, while the box around it kept its shape. The flames crackled and popped, expanding until they consumed the cardboard and caused the entire box to tip. Huge flames engulfed it, burning away the shame of that moment so long ago.

I stood silently watching until the fire went out. There was one small corner of the box that remained, so I put it into the center flame and watched as it was consumed. All that remained was a pile of gray ash. I continued staring but made no move to begin the cleanup.

I looked at Chad. "I don't know why, but I can't make myself clean it up."

"I'll do it."

"Okay." I turned and walked away.

The exercise had proved to be far more powerful than I predicted. My empty box was filled with love. My abusers were wrong, and their lies had gone up in flames.

I am powerful.

I am worthy.

I am loved.

* * *

New Year's Eve came with the dreaded reminder of resolutions not kept and new hopes dashed.

Most years I ignored the holiday and simply slept through the noise. On this night, I tossed while my brain reviewed what my abusers had done to my life. I'd weighed the pros and cons of reporting what had happened to the police. I needed to report it in case there were others who had come forward and needed another witness. I didn't want to testify or be responsible for sending anyone to jail, but I worried about the other victims Kyle and Bandit had alluded to.

I climbed out of bed, grabbed my binder of memories and drawings, and padded out to the living room.

I recorded everything in chronological order, adding dates when possible. I typed until midnight, when the noise of fireworks and celebrations intruded on my task. I brushed away the annoyance and continued, piecing everything together in a police report.

I worked until my brain and body threatened to collapse. Though I wasn't finished, I needed to stop. My battered emotions prevented me from getting the sleep I needed, so I played games on my phone until exhaustion overtook me at three in the morning.

I didn't wake until ten. I fed myself, talked to my husband for a few minutes, took a shower, and returned to my laptop. I needed to finish what I had started.

Hours later, I sat back and stared at five single-spaced typewritten pages. I wondered if I had caught the right balance between enough detail and too much detail and reviewed it for accuracy. It painted a horrific picture of abuse that continued to worsen.

I closed my laptop and looked at my husband across the small room.

"I'm done."

"How are you feeling?"

"Exhausted. Depleted."

"How so?"

I explained about the pattern of attempted rape and rape at Christmas combined with the group parties, the realization that Kyle's younger brother participated in abusing me at least eight times, the evidence of abuse occurring dozens of times with more people than I'd realized, and how seeing it all written in this way made it worse than dealing with it one incident at a time.

My husband clenched his teeth. He wanted to destroy these men. "It makes me want to reintroduce the practice of castration."

It wouldn't help. I knew from personal experience the damage other body parts and objects could inflict during abuse. The only thing that would help would be to expose their dark deeds. I had to stand up and refuse to remain a victim in the shadows. I then typed up a report for Jeff's revenge rape.

Two days later, I called the police to discover the process of reporting a crime. Knowing I had to report in the jurisdiction of where the crime was committed made my stomach protest. I had to call a small town where everyone knew each other and we had been outsiders. I wondered if they would take it seriously.

The town was so small I had trouble even finding a number. Eventually, I was transferred to a woman.

"I need to find out how to report a crime."

"What is the nature of the crime?"

"Child sexual abuse." The sound of her fingers clicking on the keyboard came through the phone.

"The perpetrator?"

"Kyle Baker."

"The address where the incident occurred?"

"I'm not sure. I'll have to get that for you."

"Date of the incident?"

"It was for two or three years sometime between 1985 and 1989."

Pause.

"And why are you reporting it now?"

"I had dissociative amnesia and just began remembering it a year a half ago. It took me this long to remember everything so I could make a statement."

"I'll have one of our detectives give you a call. It comes from a blocked number, so make sure to answer it."

"Okay." I hung up the phone.

My food refused to stay trapped in my stomach, and I ran for the bathroom. I'd only wanted to know how to report, not start a report. I wasn't ready. Then again, if I waited until I was ready, years might pass.

When the detective called, I assured him I had not reported to any other law enforcement previously, which meant it did not fall under the statute of limitations due to it being child abuse. I emailed both statements.

While I waited for the detectives to slog through the long process of investigating a case that was unlikely to result in anyone being charged, I researched trauma therapists. I needed more help than Susan could give me. I found Heather at the Trauma Treatment and Awareness Center only a half-hour drive from home. My goal was to eject every bit of my abusers from my life.

20

FAITHLESS

~~~

The memories had stayed hidden for years to keep me alive
but, paradoxically, had spread like cancer, destroying my
health, my relationships, and my happiness. Every day I walked
through a war zone, whether at church, the grocery store, or the
movies, wondering when a harmless person would shoot bullets
from their mouth to destroy my fragile psyche. All these years, I'd
never recognized the PTSD for what it was, though my therapist
in Wisconsin had tried to tell me I'd been traumatized. I wasn't
ready to accept it then. I'd probably had PTSD since I was fifteen.
I thought I was naturally anxious, overly sensitive, and depressed.
Now I knew better.

I had a variety of flashbacks ranging from split-second
fragments featuring only one of my senses, to whole memories
encompassing previous fragments. I rarely made it through a
day without something popping up. One night while brushing
my teeth, I flashed on gagging from the penis in my mouth

and knew why I had such a sensitive gag reflex. No activity was safe.

I wanted a life free from the influence of my abusers. I wanted to be me, but some days I wasn't sure who that was anymore. I wanted the flashbacks to stop. The only thing that helped was digging deeper.

In compiling the police reports, I had identified each abuser, even if I didn't know their names. My list grew from seven to ten and then to eleven when I realized there was at least one more abuser. I also stated that my abuse had started at age ten, but I hadn't moved to Hillview until I was eleven.

Once again, I pulled out my colored pencils to look deep into the murky waters through the nondominant-hand technique rather than waiting for the flashbacks to catch me off guard. My inner child refused to draw or say anything. Fear unlike any previous experience sucked me down while I wrote, "I die," over and over. I put everything away and began worrying about what lurked inside.

A couple of days later, I stood in the shower, the water coursing down my body, when I heard a man's voice quote Mormon scripture. It was the married man who occasionally popped up in my drawings but refused to become clear.

#flashback

"Reproving betimes with sharpness, when moved upon by the Holy Ghost; and then showing forth afterwards an increase of love toward him whom thou hast reproved, lest he esteem thee to be his enemy." (Doctrine and Covenants 121:43)

It wasn't until later that day I heard the rest of the story.

#memory

This adult abuser explained to me that God had told him I needed to be punished. He was only the mouthpiece. After all, "Whether by mine own voice or by the voice of my servants, it is the same." (D&C 1:38)

I sat in one of four chairs in the basement of a house. My friend Melissa sat next to me. Another ten-year-old sat to my other side, and at the end was a younger girl, around six. The man went down the row declaring, "You will be punished . . . you will service Mr. Dick." Now me, "You will be punished."

My heart sunk. I'd rather touch the body part he called Mr. Dick because it didn't hurt. To the last girl in line, he said, "You will be punished."

His words rose from the grave of my childhood: "I won't be punishing you; God will send an evil spirit to possess me to accomplish the will of the Lord."

He was Melissa's father, Mr. Wilson. He proclaimed he was the bishop of our little spiritual group of handpicked individuals chosen by his god and insisted we call him bishop while we, including his own children, were in the sacred room in his basement. If we failed to call him by his selected title, we were punished. He required restitution to God for every sin no matter how small. Confession was frequent, but sometimes he saw the evil inside me before I uttered a word.

The next day, a burning pain radiated between my legs and tiny pricks on my head reminded me of how he'd pull out my hairs a few at a time.

I pushed the memories away, compulsively completing jigsaw puzzles while listening to music or television. Anything to keep my brain from its regurgitation.

But the continued flashbacks made me accept the inevitable. I had been a victim of ritual abuse. At night I stayed up late, keeping my mind occupied until exhaustion claimed me. The memories surfaced whether I wanted them to or not.

A dark room. A locked door. Terror.

#memory

Bishop and I sat downstairs while he told me about Daniel and the lion's den. Then he opened a door and told me to go into a dark, unfinished room in his basement.

"Faith and fear can't exist at the same time. This is your lion's den, a test of your faith. The evil spirits can't hurt you if you have faith."

He shut the door, plunging me into darkness. Fear consumed me. I grasped the door, rattling the knob in my attempt to open it.

"You have to stay in there until the test is over," came his kind voice.

I backed away, unsure of what to do. Without windows, I saw only blackness. I sat next to the door on the floor, as close to the light as I could get.

A pounding on the door made me jump and move away. "Here come the evil spirits. Have faith."

Tangible darkness pressed against me, pushing me to huddle on the floor.

Did I hear something moving?

I frantically turned my head, eyes wide despite the darkness.

Something brushed against my cheek like a puff of dark wind bloated with evil.

My skin felt chilled against the cold concrete, but I didn't move.

Did I hear them whispering to me?

I don't know how long I stayed in the room—long enough the terror exhausted me. When the door opened, it hit me in the back where I lay curled in a fetal position on the floor.

"You have failed. You don't have faith. You need to be punished by God." I knew that voice. Not the kind voice of my friend's father but his alter-ego Bishop using the mean voice of the evil spirit that punished us using his body.

I got off the floor and followed him out into the basement room where the majority of our interactions occurred. Everyone else was gone. When Bishop sent them away, it was always bad news for the one left behind.

"Take your clothes off."

I looked at Mr. Wilson, but I knew if I didn't comply the punishment would be worse. I turned to go into the bathroom.

"No. Right here."

I took off my clothes one by one while he watched until I was naked. He sat me in a chair and tied my ankles to the chair legs, leaving my hands free for the things he needed me to do. He placed shallow bins of ice beneath my feet.

"For behold, when ye shall be brought to see your nakedness before God, it will kindle a flame of unquenchable fire upon you." He put something on his finger that caused horrible burning pain between my legs.

"And thus shalt thou do unto them, to cleanse them: Sprinkle water of purifying upon them." He touched burning water on symbolic parts of my body.

He did other things to hurt me, though nothing that left a mark my parents or teachers might see. I did anything he asked me to do to prevent worse pain.

Finally, he stopped. "It is finished. God is satisfied."

"Put your clothes on." The kind voice returned. "Do you want a soda?"

"Okay." I untied the cloth strips and put my clothing on, glad to be covered.

We returned upstairs where I drank my soda while we watched a movie. His children, my friends, returned from getting ice cream and joined us in front of the television. That's where we were when Mom finally came to pick me up.

Bits and pieces continued to surface over the next few months. No matter how I tried as a child, I was never good enough. I was punished by Bishop for not sharing with my brother, for not listening to my mother the first time she asked, and for thinking unkind thoughts. Through it all, we were required to remain silent no matter what happened.

Bishop abused me at least once a week for nine months. Only once did he tell me God had no punishment, but I still had to service Mr. Dick.

I never told anyone. A fragment of a flashback helped me understand why. He said my mother knew I had been chosen and was happy about it. My anger now burned that he'd lied to me about my mother approving what he did. The other abuse I'd uncovered was child's play compared to the evil of this monster.

Horrific pain radiated from my chest until I wanted to get out Chad's gun and shoot a hole into my heart to stop it.

When Chad returned home from work and I told him he needed to remove the gun. He used the second locking mechanism on our safe and kept the key with him until he could move it to his dad's safe. Two weeks later, he still hadn't removed it.

"You need to get rid of the gun."

"I always have the key with me, so you can't get into the safe even if you wanted to."

"I can get the key. I'm aware of every time you are in the garage or in the shower and don't have your keys with you. You have to take the gun away before it's too late."

He took the gun and drove it to his parents' house that night.

I tried to stop the memories even though I knew I needed to deal with them. They were too difficult to face, too filled with evil.

Flashes of a council of judgment bubbled up. The men involved were part of a larger group where they did not get the recognition or status they felt they deserved. They faithfully attended, but Mr. Wilson established a smaller group in his home. A stranger sat on his left while one of his neighbors sat on his right. A council always consisted of four, and they needed another, so they pulled in one of Mr. Wilson's older sons. He had survived his own purification and was being rewarded for his faithfulness.

I sat before the council of judgment. The first order of business was to decide on my punishment for trying to resist when Bishop wanted to hurt me near the beginning of my nine-month nightmare.

I had said, "I want to go play outside." I got up from my chair in line and moved several steps toward the stairs.

#memory

Bishop declared to the council that I had tried to run away, which proved I was not humble and submissive.

The council agreed I must be punished for my disobedience and bow down before god in humility to declare my nothingness.

One of the men commanded me to remove my clothes to acknowledge my nakedness before god. Then he led me to a small box with holes on the sides. He ordered me to climb in and kneel down. He forced me to bend over my knees and closed the box over my head, resting something on it to prevent me from getting out.

Through the holes on the side, Melissa's older brother and the stranger poked sticks at me. The neighbor I knew from church banged on the side of the box. Bishop yelled out things I needed to say to repent before God.

"Tell God you are nothing!"

"I am nothing."

"Louder!"

"I am nothing!"

"For dust thou art and unto dust shalt thou return. What are you?"

"I am dust."

When they finally lifted the lid, I began standing until my legs buckled. I stood more slowly and stepped out of the box. I knelt on the floor with two men beside me to keep me in line and submissive.

Bishop took one of his daughter's baby dolls, placed it on the floor between us and declared it stood as a sacrifice just as Isaac was spared by the ram in the thicket.

He plunged a knife into its chest and cut downward, creating a line from heart to stomach.

He mumbled evil, Satanic words somewhat similar to an incantation.

With a broken stick, he scratched a line in the same spot along my chest and stomach, then used the burning holy water to anoint my scratch and purify it. It hurt, causing silent tears to escape. I dared not make a sound, for they warned further punishments for not enduring the wrath of god.

I was required to offer up repentance and restitution to god, and then to Bishop, whom I had hurt by my disobedience.

My memory breaks into fragments here. I remember a bee sting in my upper arm which now I know was a needle. Dim shadows of being punished to the edge of endurance. A clear shard emerged of me pretending to be a dog on the floor right before Bishop's adult body ripped into my tiny one in a pain-filled rape.

Eventually the shadows solidified into real people again as the drugs wore off. I didn't know if the rape was one of the last things to happen as I came out of my haze or just painful enough to be imprinted in my mind despite it.

Eventually the memory became completely clear again when we sat down on the floor, kneeling toward each other with his clothes zipped and tucked properly while I knelt naked and small in front of him.

"We have completed our sacred rituals. God is satisfied. We do not talk of sacred things outside of this holy room. Do not talk of the purification to anyone."

He lifted my chin with his finger and gazed into my eyes. I had to look up as he towered over me even on the floor. "Your mother knows you are being purified. She is happy you have been chosen. Even between a mother and her daughter you must not talk of the sacred things we do here. I spoke to her here, where it is permitted because this space has been purified. She assures me you will be able to keep sacred things private. Outside this room you are coming to a playdate with Melissa, understand?"

"Yes," I whispered.

Anger churned the contents of my stomach until I ran to the bathroom and threw up. No wonder I thought my mother hadn't loved me as a child. Having these new details of exactly what he'd said caused further pain. Only once had I resisted going to the weekly playdates. I didn't remember the details of what happened but it was severe enough I never missed again. If Chad hadn't removed the handgun, I would have found a way to use it.

For weeks I tried to remember the first name of the man who abused me. There were hundreds of Wilsons in Utah and thousands in the United States, even narrowing it down by his approximate age. At church it was Brother Wilson, and in his basement, we had to call him Bishop. Someone must have called him by his first name around me, but it remained elusive.

Men who abused tended to continue until they were caught. This evil man was probably out there abusing other girls and women. My mother remembered hearing that Mr. Wilson had been charged with the sexual abuse of his daughters. We both searched but came up empty-handed. Neither of us remembered a name or could find any articles about someone from the tiny town being charged with child abuse.

I searched the inmate list for the Utah prison system, but no males with the last name of Wilson were the right age.

On a Monday night, I decided to drive with my husband the ninety minutes to the town where my abuse happened to locate the house and discover the name of the man by his address. When we got off the freeway and headed toward the town, knots began to form in my stomach. After more than thirty years, it was unsettlingly familiar.

I knew the ranch-style house was near the small church. Only two houses fit what I remembered. One house I barely looked at, rejecting it outright. Though we drove farther, I assumed the only other house must be it.

I looked at the little church and knew I'd been abused there as well. I remembered playing in the small community park adjacent to the church.

Chad and I snapped a few pictures of the town and drove out to the house where I had lived. I handled it without feeling anxious or upset, unlike when I'd returned to Hillview to see my house, Kyle's house, and the shed I'd lived in. My lack of emotion should have been my first clue that something wasn't right.

The next day, Mom called, telling me she and Dad were driving to the town to identify the house they had taken me to play at every week all those years ago.

Dad drove past the house I'd picked, but Mom knew it wasn't the right one. He drove to the other house, the one I'd barely looked at and dismissed.

"This is the house. I'm sure of it. Did you get pictures when you were here?"

"Not of that house, and I forgot to take a picture of the church. Can you have Dad take pictures of each of them?"

While Dad took the pictures, I stayed on the phone with my mother.

"This is just creepy," Mom said.

"I was fine before, but now my anxiety is going crazy, which tells me this must be the right house. We drove by, and I barely looked at it. I probably couldn't face seeing it."

"I want to throw up looking at this house."

I stayed quiet, struggling with my urge to vomit. The more I pictured the house, the more certain I became that it was the house where I had been abused. I hung up to escape.

With an address, I found Mr. Wilson in less than an hour. He was the right age and had been to prison for child sexual assault. I stared at the pictures I was able to pull up online. When I had enough information, I wrote up another police report and submitted it to the detective who was handling my case.

More memories surfaced. I was no longer shocked by the things I remembered but cried for the little girl trying to survive, for the pain, and for the injustice of being hurt by a trusted church member.

I marveled at the resilience of that young version of myself. She had known what they were doing was wrong. She'd obeyed and dissociated in order to survive, but she had survived.

21

LOSING MY RELIGION

Pain plunged into my heart and broke into shards that raced through my body, leaving carnage in their wake. The first casualty was my religion.

Bishop had wielded scripture like a scalpel and used it not to heal but to harm me. Concepts were molded to have different meanings, crafted to blend with teachings at church and embed lies deeply into my psyche.

I'd followed my religion with exactness while viewing God more as an abuser waiting to punish me rather than a merciful and forgiving being. I was seen by others as righteous, faithful, and strong in the way I followed everything I thought God asked of me, which solidified my convoluted view.

I'd rarely attended church even before I remembered what Mr. Wilson had done because of the minefield of triggers there. Now I wasn't sure if I even believed in God.

It was Sunday again, and Chad attended church with two of my children. I often kept busy cleaning but couldn't focus today. Instead, I sat at my desk and stared at the wall.

Questions rolled around in my head. The most pressing was, what if God wasn't who I thought?

I'd studied other religions and knew the various versions of God they believed in. What if one of their versions was right and I was wrong? Or what if we were all a little right and a little wrong, creating God into what we wanted? If we all created our own versions, did that make God mad, or was that all a part of his plan, to be everything we needed him to be?

God might not have instructed me to take on one hard thing after another. I might have heaped it all on myself, dancing to the echoes of my abuse.

I put my head in my hands and let that thought settle. My abusers had taught me that I wasn't good enough, that I needed to earn love, and that my own wants and needs didn't matter. I'd walked through life trying to prove myself. And what better way to prove myself than take on difficult things? I'd been taught life was hard. I figured it was better to choose for myself rather than wait for God or nature to knock me down. I'd also been taught God wanted me to have joy.

What was true and what was false?

Mr. Wilson had twisted scripture and used it as justification for abuse. While it took a sick mind to do what he had done, it showed me how easy it is to create our own meaning from scripture. I'd been taught it was my responsibility to be guided by the Holy Spirit to know what was true and what wasn't. If I couldn't distinguish the programming from my abusers from the truth, how could I trust whisperings from the Spirit that might instead be created in my faulty brain?

My brain recreated flashbacks as if they happened in real-time, even giving me physical sensations and sounds. God might be a figment of my imagination.

The hardness of the chair beneath me reminded me I was an adult sitting in my office, but inside I was a lost child in a big and confusing world. I got up and turned on the television to drown out my thoughts.

When I lost my faith, I lost my community. When I stopped showing up to church and the many activities they sponsored, I was treated by my neighbors almost like they forgot I existed. I had one friend who kept in contact with me, but other than that, communication from the community I'd lived in for eleven years was rare.

My angry outbursts, my lashing out against Mormon culture and the teachings I viewed as incorrect, or against Mormons who'd damaged me hurt my sweet husband. He treated me with kindness and love, refused to be swayed from his beliefs, and allowed me the space to work out my own belief system. It was the best possible reaction to my inner struggle.

I fought for my faith in God. Even if I never trusted organized religion again, I needed a connection to God. It only took a few weeks for me to realize that I believed to the core of my soul that God existed. The memories of the sweetness of his love for mankind, and more specifically of me, were stronger than the lies Bishop had woven through me.

I needed to get away from the pressures at home to reconnect with God. My Mom and Dad were leaving town for theweekend, so I worked it out to go to their condo for the quiet. I told everyone except Chad that it was my birthday present to myself, an overnight stay away from the kids. Life without God wasn't a life worth living. I knew he was not a figment of my imagination, a crutch, or faulty wiring in my brain.

At first I avoided what I'd driven ninety minutes to accomplish. I read from a novel and watched a movie.

When the sun set, I reluctantly knelt to pray. I knew God understood how angry I was, but I let it all pour out anyway. I talked out loud about the betrayal of those who'd abused me while they pretended to follow Him. Every mean word, uncomfortable look, and unfair comment seemed to roll through my memory, and my expressions of anger and hurt continued. I pleaded with Him to talk to me, let me feel Him close again, and guide me to know what to do.

I ended by saying, "I am here, listening, and finally ready to hear whatever you want me to know."

I believe God communicates with us in the way we are most comfortable. For me, it is by writing out the words. When I'd wondered years ago if the thoughts in my head were from me or God, I wrote them down. The words didn't sound like me, and from then on I began typing out the words that enter my mind.

So I waited in the dark, my laptop sitting in front of me with the screen dimmed. Scriptures began filling my mind.

"Therefore, was the wrath of the Lord kindled against his people." (Psalms 106, King James Version).

"There be some that trouble you and would pervert the gospel of Christ." (Galatians 1:7)

"Woe unto them that call evil good and good evil; that put darkness for light and light for darkness." (Isaiah 5:20)

"Then said he unto the disciples, it is impossible but that offences will come: but woe unto him through whom they come! It were better for him that a millstone were hanged about his neck, and he cast into the sea than that he should offend one of these little ones." (Luke 17:1–2)

God didn't try to tell me not to be angry, the first thing he did was acknowledge my anger by showing me his anger, along with examples that the world was filled with those who chose evil.

The word of the Lord flowed through me and out my fingertips onto the page.

You are angry with me, but your anger is nothing compared to the wrath of a perfect God on the wicked. My children whom I loved have turned against me, defiled my world which I created for them, and perverted the paths of righteousness.

"I am the good shepherd: the good shepherd giveth his life for the sheep. My sheep hear my voice, and I know them, and they follow me." (John 10:11, 27)

I am the Lord God Almighty and my word is law. My promises are sure else I would cease to be God. Have I not promised you eternal life? Don't focus on the struggle, the sacrifice, without remembering the blessings, the joy to come for those who follow me.

I wrestled within myself. I didn't want to let go of my anger yet. The injustices played across my mind: the abuse, financial struggle, depression, illness, my desire to be a good mom and failing over and over again. I paused in agony.

And then I saw my home covered in flames, as if in a dream. These flames didn't burn like earthly fire but had a purity to them. While the house was not consumed, the people inside were. The painful fire burned their souls rather than their bodies. I wanted to run and save them from the pain, but I knew it was a good fire, a refining fire, something bringing change.

The fire stopped, causing my family inside to fall to the ground gasping. I saw that I was among them, writhing in pain. I was helpless to alleviate their pain, but I knew when it stopped they would stand as strong, new beings.

My family and I began to glow, light coming from within, enough to light the entire house and send rays bursting through the windows for all to see, beacons in the noble fight against evil. The image faded away.

I will watch over you. I will knit your family back together, stronger than you could imagine. Don't abandon your children, just hold them in your hands, pray over them. When they leave the nest, they fall for a moment but then they learn to fly.

I was wrapped in the Spirit of God. He'd wept as I was being abused, his heart had cried out in pain as I'd struggled and walked away. He'd experienced everything that had happened to me and never left me alone.

My heart broke again, letting the anger fall away, leaving me vulnerable as the pain washed through me.

I prayed again, thanking the Creator of the universe for all he had given me and asking for the things my family and I needed. A parade of moments when God had helped me passed by, things I had never noticed or understood before that moment.

The distance between God and His child was breached. I didn't know how long it would last; after all, I was a flawed human. None are perfect but God, who allows frail human beings to be his hands and feet here on the earth in learning to help others.

The next day I returned home, rested and at peace. I let Chad know he could bring his gun back to store it in our safe. It made me feel safe knowing it was there if anyone broke into the house. I wish I could say that one experience stayed with me and kept me from further problems and questions, but it did not. Life rushed in again, bringing doubts with it, but I pressed forward.

With a renewed desire to attend church, I returned, but so did my flashbacks. This time it was during the sacramental prayers.

#flashback

Mr. Wilson nudged a knife into his inner arm, creating a short, shallow cut. Blood welled up, and when there was enough, he pressed his thumb into the blood and then anointed my forehead with it.

"I have sacrificed for you, for you can only be cleansed with the blood of the righteous and I am the only righteous man present. Bow, kiss the wounds of my flesh, and thank me for the sacrifice I have made for you."

Now, sitting in the pew at church, I felt the blood on my forehead. I discreetly rubbed my hand across the spot, hoping to erase the sensation. As soon as my fingers left my skin, the phantom touch returned.

I looked around to distract myself, and my eyes settled on two little girls with blonde ponytails. One was about ten, the other, sitting a couple rows forward, was younger.

I fought the urge to snatch them up and hide them to protect them from getting hurt. It grew into an obsession. I didn't know where the abusers hid among the congregants; all I saw was more children to be harmed.

I walked out of the chapel, unable to ground myself in the present until I returned home.

Each week, I fought to attend despite the pain it caused me to be there. Sunday school lessons triggered memories of the Satanic rituals, and I'd have to get up and leave. Talks from the pulpit, prayers, and overheard conversations pushed me into battles waged within my head.

On the outside I looked like any other woman sitting in a dress. Inside I was a battle-weary soldier in an endless war, wounded but still fighting with help from God. Some days held victories, but most ended in stalemates or setbacks.

The Mormon religion is built of lay leaders, meaning no one is paid. Rather than sermons, talks are given by congregants. Once a month, we fast, and anyone in the audience can go to the podium and share their testimony, in a belief that not only does the speaker grow by expressing their faith but the listeners as well.

As I shared my testimony, it became entangled in the abuse, and in testifying of the reality of God in my journey, I inadvertently shared too much. I was asked not to speak of abuse in settings where children were present. I was humiliated and upset, but it didn't take long to get over it, because I knew it was inappropriate. What settled deep in my heart was that I no longer belonged within the conservative Mormon community. I was different now.

Few noticed the change within me or the fact that I moved from attending as my mental health allowed to no attendance at all.

No other religions appealed to me, so I decided to be a nondenominational Christian. I had my faith in God, and for now, that was enough.

Months later, I realized that just as the wheat and tares (an injurious weed) had grown together in order not to destroy the wheat when pulling the weeds, the incorrect teachings of my abusers had grown with the truth. Though the field looked like a tangled mess, the farmer was able to separate out the wheat from the tares at harvest (see Matthew 13:24–30).

I needed to separate the truth from the lies, so I created a pyramid and listed my beliefs on each layer. I defined what each item meant to me. Next, I created an inverted pyramid with the beliefs I struggled with and why.

In trauma therapy, I gathered the tares into bundles and burned them. At home, I gathered the wheat and stored it in my heart.

Don't believe that the process was easy or quick. It took time, effort, and loving support. As any farmer knows, the work is never-ending. God constantly gives me new good seeds and teaches me how to spot and remove the weeds. I had no idea how vital that learning would become in the final battles I needed to win.

22

RAPID PAIN
RELEASE

A buse breeds loneliness. Barriers divided me from those who had happy childhoods, who seemed afraid of the darkness I could no longer keep hidden. Some wanted to ignore it, pretending that horrible things didn't happen. Others looked at me with pity, worry, or condemnation that I was no longer attending church. All I could do was try to survive.

As I tried to understand the depth of what had happened to me, I searched for information on the internet. I found evidence of widespread ritualistic abuse in Utah in the eighties. I wasn't alone.

I googled the definition of ritual abuse and read, "the alleged sexual abuse or murder of people, especially children, supposedly committed as part of satanic rituals."

Words like *alleged* and *supposedly* jumped off the page and slapped me in the face. Websites blamed media for the false panic of Satanic abuse in the eighties and early nineties and shared findings that reports of this type of abuse were a myth. I knew it was no myth.

I narrowed my search to what had happened in Utah and discovered that a huge investigation had uncovered a therapist who was proven to have planted memories in her patients. This, along with a lack of physical evidence, caused them to conclude that the stories of abuse were created by unscrupulous therapists.

I wanted to scream at that therapist for what she had done. The patients had probably experienced abuse, but due to her mishandling, they were further traumatized, along with everyone else who experienced ritual abuse and wasn't believed. The media had further hurt the victims by sensationalizing the stories until few accepted the accounts. Fury lit my veins on fire.

My memories came out at home, and then I would tell my therapists about them. I couldn't recall a single time where they'd tried to put any words in my mouth. Their job was to help me cope with what I was unlocking. I knew that despite my creativity, there was no way I was capable of making up the sickening things I had drawn.

I kept searching, trying to find a support group or better information to understand my abuse. It wasn't until I found a website from the United Kingdom that I began to make sense of the hype, the myths, and the truth (see https://information. pods-online.org.uk/demystifying-ritual-abuse/).

It laid out a clear definition of what ritual abuse was, why it was declared a myth, and what types of things commonly happened within it.

It stated that not all ritual abuse was Satanic, and while many victims developed multiple-personality disorder, others

226

did not. It depended on the age when the abuse started, the severity, the duration, and the coping skills. I had dissociated to survive but hadn't been diagnosed with multiple-personality disorder. Now I knew why. I was older when the abuse began, it lasted less than a year, and I had a family to go home to.

Along with information that made sense, the website spoke of the possibility of healing. I'd finally found a website that was built on information rather than on sensationalized stories attempting to sway the reader to one side or the other. My heart told me healing was possible.

When I read that ritual abuse was "robbing a person of their free will," the truth sunk in. Yes. This was what they had done. I'd had no choice. If I didn't do what they wanted, the punishment was severe, the only way to survive was to comply.

As I read through the list of characteristics, my mind automatically cued up memories that matched the descriptions. *Forced Perpetration:* Mr. Wilson forced his son to assist in torture or be hurt himself. *Psychological Abuse:* threats and lies kept me silent. *Double Binds:* compliance or unbearable torture. *Lies, Tricks, & Technology:* "Your mother knows and is happy that you have been chosen." *Forced to Take Drugs:* the sting in my arm followed by blackouts of time. *Non-Human Dissociative Parts/Alters:* sending demons to haunt me; crouching on all fours while Bishop held my ponytail like a leash. *Use of Restraints and Confinement:* cramped in boxes; shut in dark closets and rooms. *Torture, Especially Kinds that Don't Leave Marks on the Body:* pain, more pain than I could handle. *Forced Participation in Child Pornography, Prostitution, and Sex Trafficking:* I don't remember, I don't know.

My body rocked back and forth. I clicked to scroll down past worse abuse, worried that reading about them might trigger new memories. I tried to look away, but I'd already seen *Mind Control,* which reminded me of how I'd scoffed that such a thing was possible before I remembered my abuse.

One last line jumped out at me: *Sudden Impulsive Desires to Self-Harm or Attempt Suicide.* No, Bishop never programmed me to kill myself if I talked about my abuse. I'd spent years feeling suicidal but never followed through.

Near the bottom, another item caught my attention. It listed chronic pain as a characteristic, especially when undiagnosable. The article stated that the pain was a memory of what the body had previously experienced during the trauma. Maybe my paralysis was a body memory of not being able to move from the drugs. I dismissed that thought, but I'd read too much to dismiss everything.

I'd suffered for more than thirty years from what my abusers had done to me. I hated them, but also didn't want to expend any more energy on them.

I closed my laptop, pulled out a puzzle, and turned on the television. My brain had long ago admitted that I'd been ritualistically abused, but matching the items with my list made it devastatingly real.

Ritual abuse wasn't a myth or an exaggeration. There were people all over the world and right in my own city who had come forward but had been ridiculed and rejected.

For days I struggled, trying to grapple with the depth and reality of my abuse. I forgot for hours at a time in order to survive, while some days I barely functioned. It didn't help that I heard back from the detective assigned to my case. Without a living witness or confession from any of the perpetrators they interviewed, there was no way to move forward without any forensic evidence. Rationally, I understood and even expected this news, but my heart still hurt as if somehow the police didn't believe my story. My case was officially inactive and would stay that way until the statute of limitations closed it.

Eventually, I regained my equilibrium enough to notice something out of balance in my body.

I'd become used to doing energy work with Chad ever since he'd used it to help me during my time in the wheelchair. On a Saturday afternoon while the kids were occupied, I turned to him. "Can you do more energy work? Something is wrong with my heart."

"Okay."

I lay down, and he began feeling my energy. I'd learned that for the sessions to be productive, I needed to focus as much as he was. Eyes closed, I became aware of my heart—not my physical heart but the battered and torn heart of my soul. It looked deflated, detached, and almost dead.

I had no idea how to fix it, causing me to return to the trapped little girl filled with pain. Bishop was still too elusive for Little Dawn to find, so she turned to Kyle and pounded her fists into his chest as he smugly looked down at someone who could never hurt him.

Adult Dawn moved toward Little Dawn and took her by the hand. "It's okay. I'm going to protect you. I won't let anything else bad happen to you."

With the retreat of anger came a wave of pain that filled me with indignation. Adult Dawn became powerful, expanding and pushing a circle of energy that rippled outward, knocking over

Kyle and his band of abusive friends and disintegrating the house where the abuse happened. Adult Dawn continued expanding, becoming more powerful and large, absorbing Little Dawn within her. Kyle floated above his house, trapped in an invisible bubble.

I looked down on the small houses and noticed how small Kyle was now. Dragging Kyle in his bubble behind me, I flew to the tiny town where Mr. Wilson resided. I reached out my hand and commanded him to come out of hiding. Up through the roof of one of the houses floated an old man.

I pointed to him and told my Creator, "That is the man who abused me. I stand as a witness against him."

I turned to another town, where Bandit resided. He had moved away, but a string of light sucked him back and then he also floated up. With a mere thought, I pulled the three floating abusers together in front of me, raised my head to the heavens, and turned my palm up to God. "I stand as a witness against these men and bring them before you." They were pulled up to the heavens and out of sight.

I stood hundreds of feet in the air and looked around. "I call all the victims of these men to rise." Spirits rose all over Utah, while others appeared across the United States.

"I am your voice. I will stand as a witness for you. I will be here to help you." The many who rose up were recorded by angels as witnesses against the three men who had gone to be judged of God.

My body jerked as I returned to awareness of my physical body.

I noticed it was only those three men I needed to bear witness against, none of the other twelve. These were the men I knew had abused others. I needed to be a voice for those victims, though I had no idea how to do that.

Later that week in trauma therapy, my therapist, Heather, began something called Rapid Pain Release. First, she helped me relax. I stood looking out at the ocean. She had me imagine taking steps downward, each step helping me become more relaxed.

At the bottom of the steps, she gave me a moment to enjoy the beach before I walked down a path to a tree. She told me there was a girl standing under the tree, but I saw four girls.

They were my inner children. The youngest was the innocent girl before the abuse. Her shoulder-length blonde hair shone almost as much as the joy in her eyes. I gave her a hug, as instructed by my therapist, filling her with love.

Next was the child who'd experienced the ritual abuse. She and I both knew it wasn't her fault. I sorrowed for what she experienced and gave her a hug as well. I was proud of how she'd found a way to survive.

The third girl had hair stretching down her back, hair she loved, though I had lost that piece of myself. I looked into her eyes, finally being able to tell her I knew it wasn't her fault. I no longer blamed her for returning to Kyle. I knew the power he held over her. I hugged her and tried to fill her with my love as well.

I turned to the fourth girl, the sullen teen with a pixie cut and pain-filled eyes.

"I'm sorry I blamed you all these years."

She looked down, not trusting me yet.

"You were filled with pain without knowing what happened to you and where it came from. You knew something was wrong, and you did your best. Your best was good enough. You stayed alive so I could experience an amazing life. I'm sorry I've blamed you and hated you all these years. I didn't understand."

I hugged her, and she clung to me. She let go, looked down, and moved back. I needed to keep walking, but at least she held a glimmer of peace.

Heather instructed me to walk to a large meadow. Once there she said, "Take all the packets of pain inside you and leave them here in the meadow."

The amount of pain overwhelmed me. I picked up a large sack and sagged under its weight. I dropped it on the ground and then took another, heaving it on top of the first. Tired already, I knew it was hopeless to move them all.

"I'm overwhelmed. There's too much pain," I told Heather.

"You don't have to do it yourself. Think of all those you love—family and friends—and let them come and help you."

I began imagining them, but I knew it would take too long, even with their help, and I wasn't sure I wanted them there. Instead, I called on God. I asked him to burn away my pain.

A bright light shone into my chest and moved through my body, burning away the darkness that dwelled inside me.

Bits of dark ash remained, so I asked God to wash it away. A concentrated stream of water washed my body, beginning at my head and moving down to my feet. I imagined hinges on my toes, which I opened up to let the dirty water rush out into the meadow.

My brain needed an even more concentrated spray to get into the folds and recesses of my brain. God moved down one side, then shifted to a different angle to get to any hidden pockets, and washed again from the back. Three passes rid my brain of the darkness my abusers had filled my head with. No darkness remained.

"I'm finished," I told Heather.

"Do you see the pile of pain?"

I turned, and there it was—a huge pile of filth at least a foot taller than I was. "Yes."

"Here we have cans of gasoline and flamethrowers."

I grinned.

"Pour the gasoline on the pile and use the flame thrower to light it on fire."

I poured the gas and lit it on fire.

"Tell me when the pile is finished burning."

The fire burned slowly. I knew I didn't have enough time during our session to wait, so again I turned to God, asking Him to incinerate it for me. Like Superman, he shot twin lasers from his eyes at the pile, and it disappeared, leaving a tiny pile of gray dust. A puff of wind picked up the dust and scattered it into nothing.

Finished, my therapist walked me back the way I had come, and soon I had opened my eyes. Air flowed not only into my lungs but through my entire body, breezing through spaces no longer clogged with darkness.

In another session, we visited the Place of the Rocks, where I returned the pain I carried for others. Only then could I go to the cabin.

At the cabin, Heather had me invite all the parts of my personality to be present. One by one they showed up: Joyful and Playful first, then Creative, Confident, Strength, and Honesty. Anger sulked in with Goth Girl, followed by Maternal Love, while Hectic rushed in last. I looked around and noticed Shy in the corner. Disease slumped on the sofa as if she'd been there for hours. Twelve parts of my personality resided in one place, like girls forced by their parents to attend a meeting.

"What parts of your personality are holding pain for you?" Heather asked.

"Shy, Goth Girl, Hectic, and Disease. Shy is holding the pain of all the embarrassing and hurtful things that happened to me at school. Hectic has the judgments of others. She tries to please everyone but never seems to please anyone. Goth Girl holds Kyle and his friends and the pain from high school, trying to cope with being blamed for something she didn't do. Disease is holding the ritual abuse." I shuddered at the ugliness of Disease. "Disease has leprosy, with patches of skin hanging off; she's old and wrinkled, with gray hair falling out from chemotherapy."

"Would they like to let go of the pain they are holding for you?"

"Shy will, but the rest are scared. They want to wait and see what is going to happen first."

"Hold out your hand," Heather said. I held it out, and she clasped it. "I'm going to pull the pain out through your hand. Keep grasping my hand until all the pain is gone. While that is happening, I'm going to fill you with light by touching you on your arm. This will create balance and allow the pain to leave." Her other hand rested on my forearm.

"Are you ready?" Heather asked.

"Yes."

Her hand tightened in mine with a slight pull away from my body. Like maple running down a tap, my pain slid down the sluice of my arm and out of my body while light was sucked in to fill the void. Time held no meaning as I focused only on accepting and observing the process. When all the pain was released, I let go of her hand.

"Now the others want to go."

"We're out of time, but tell them we will get rid of their pain in our next session." Heather walked me out of the cabin, away from my personalities, and eventually back to awareness.

Over the next week, I adjusted to the lightness inside. Things were good, and I didn't want to upset the balance by facing Disease again. That aspect of my personality scared me, so I spent my next session talking about my life.

A week later, Heather took me back to the cabin. Hectic and Goth Girl released their pain. Disease stepped forward. As we began the process, a massive darkness poured out of her, as if she had carried a piece of hell within her. When the last of it drained out, Disease was transformed. Her hair and skin were restored; long golden waves surrounded a flawless face. Light grew within her until it shone through her translucent skin.

"My purpose is complete," she said. "It was my job to hold the darkness so it wouldn't consume you until you were ready and able to deal with it."

She turned and dissolved into bits of light that streaked to the heavens in a column of sparks.

With my work in the cabin complete, I closed and locked the door. Heather helped me return, and our entire hour was up.

"That was a lot of pain you were carrying," Heather commented.

"I know, but it's gone."

"How do you feel?"

"Really light, like, not only filled with light but as if I don't weigh as much. It's weird."

"You've let go of a huge burden," Heather said.

I left with hope in my heart that filled the emptiness inside with light. I treasured each piece of healing, longing for each to be the last, but knew that complex trauma required as many layers to heal as layers of pain I discovered hidden within.

23

SCOTLAND

After years of hiding at home, it was scary to step into the possibility of my dreams, but taking the opportunities life presented opened the world to me.

For six months, I went through the Calliope Inner Circle Writing Program and was exposed to Angie on a regular basis. It was unlike anything I'd ever experienced. I learned the craft of writing, but that was only a portion of what Angie taught.

Angie believed in me before I believed in myself. She listened, pushed, and gave tough love when necessary. She taught me how to move from daydreaming to creating a path to accomplishing my dreams. She gave me space to discover the power I held within myself.

The person I'd buried years ago began to emerge. I'd been curious, charismatic, and full of joy before my abusers had intruded in my life and stolen my childhood. Those traits merged with the empathy, patience, and wisdom I'd gained as an adult. I learned how to dream, accept my strengths and flaws, and constantly stretch myself.

I made a new set of friends who were writers also going through the program. These friends were different, more supportive and loving of who I was and the difficult road I travelled on my healing journey.

When I completed the course, I stayed on with a few of my new friends to be a writing coach for the next group and continued experiencing positive breakthroughs. I stepped into the world with confidence and created positive connections. Randi and I worked together assisting Angie and created a bond of friendship and trust.

One day, Angie announced a writing retreat in Scotland. It made no sense financially or with Gavin coming home from the hospital after almost a year in residential treatment, but I knew I had to be there. I'd spent years researching my husband's ancestors in the area and discovered that the castle we would be staying at was mere miles from where the ancestors I'd researched were born and lived before emigrating to America.

I'd never been out of the country and rarely traveled except to visit family, but Chad and I decided to go. We planned an extra couple of days so Chad could show me London. He'd been there on a work trip years earlier.

We put the whole thing on a credit card, something rare for us. Gavin moved home, and six weeks later my mother picked him up to stay with her while we were gone.

I climbed onto a huge plane for the nonstop flight from Salt Lake City to London in a cloud of disbelief and stepped off in a new country in a haze of jet lag. I decided to ignore the jet lag, let the problems slide off me, and experience all this trip had to offer me. Heathrow was a complex maze unlike any other airport I'd been in, but, surprisingly, it didn't faze me. A small shuttle drove us out to the tarmac, where we boarded a tiny plane to Edinburgh. An hour later, we stepped off into the cool, humid air of Scotland.

While Chad focused on driving on the left side of the road, I was able to drink in the sights around me. I'd spent forty years avoiding new things. Vacations caused my anxiety to spike, and I longed only to go home. Now, in a foreign country with little sleep, I let every new sight and experience wash over me.

We picked up another guest, grabbed some lunch, and headed north into the Scottish Highlands. Off the freeway system, the roads were narrow, so I focused on the rolling green fields dotted with sheep and lined with darker mounds of trees. Edinburgh held quaint old buildings packed tightly together, but the open spaces of the Scottish Highlands gave me room to breathe. We finally rounded a bend, and Forter Castle came into view.

"It's so tall and skinny!" I exclaimed.

The others laughed at my delight. It didn't matter how many pictures I'd seen of the world; nothing compared to being here. Where some castles were huge and squat, our castle stood tall on a small rise, tiny turrets jutting out from the top level giving ancient inhabitants a vantage point for spotting danger. The late-evening sun bathed the stones in warm light. These stones had endured attacks and fires, standing strong after 450 years, far longer than America had been a country.

My feet dug into the thick gravel driveway as I walked to the heavy wooden door, where I turned an ancient iron ring and stepped into the past. Stone steps led down into the kitchen and up into the main hall, where furniture was stuffed into every nook and cranny, with narrow walkways between the large sofas, chairs, and a long dining table.

We continued past the room to the tiny spiral staircase that wound upward to the guest rooms. It was hard to believe that the girl who'd spent years daydreaming of a trip to Hawaii had instead jumped across the pond. I immersed myself in every experience, from the sound of the bleating sheep through my narrow window in the morning to navigating the local marketplace in search of items on Angie's list. Angie had arrived early to prepare, but instead became quite ill. She confined herself to the Laird's bedroom and sent the guests off to explore Scotland without her.

The first item on our personal agenda was visiting the places mentioned in Chad's great-great-grandfather's diary written entirely in poetry. Thomas Frazer was known as Utah's Robert Browning and was an accomplished brick mason by trade. We started in Dunkeld, where his older siblings had been born, and followed Blairgowrie Road to Clunie, the birthplace of Thomas. The parish stood up the bank from Loch of Clunie, with only a couple of houses nearby. It was a place forgotten by time. As we walked through the cemetery, we found the graves of his ancestors and felt their presence and profound gratitude that they were not forgotten. Though related only by marriage, I had researched this particular line and felt deeply connected to them. Their presence grounded me and reminded me that I was part of a larger whole with greater purpose than my own struggles.

The next day we followed the group to Doune Castle, where Monty Python and the Holy Grail and Outlander were filmed. I let go of my self-consciousness and reenacted the storming of the castle with coconut halves purchased at the gift shop while my writing friend, Randi filmed us. On our way back, we stopped to try haggis, a dish containing sheep's lung, heart, and liver minced and formed to create something resembling meatloaf. It tasted good as long as I didn't think about what it contained.

With Angie still sick, Chad and I drove across the Scottish Highlands to a respected baker in Forfar, where bridies, or Scottish meat pastries, were invented. I enjoyed the lush countryside, content to ride alone with Chad.

"You're different this trip," Chad said.

"How?"

"I haven't had to apologize for anything."

I laughed and looked at him. I wasn't sure what he meant.

"Usually you are miserable, and I'm apologizing for everything, but you're enjoying this trip. I was worried about how you would handle it."

"I guess that's true. I decided to let all that stuff go and have fun. When am I ever going to get to come here again?"

"I like it."

"Me too." It was true. Until this year, I only remembered negative things about the trips we'd taken. I'd barely slept in the drafty cabin when we'd gone to a reunion in Yellowstone and remembered only the horrible bed and desperately wanting to go home. Easter at my mom's in Florida brought memories of Calvin having a panic attack and me staying behind with three-year-old Nicole since I thought she was too young for Disney World. Mom lived there for seven years and despite several trips out there, I never went to Disney World. How many other opportunities had I missed?

I'd spent my life afraid to live, waiting for bad things to happen. Here in Scotland, our fearless leader was sick, and cars got in accidents. The well was running dry, and the laundry was always wet.

Smells emerged from the toilets, and showers were accompanied by a racket of machinery. Nothing went as planned, but I had fun anyway.

Though I had intended to be a guest, I stepped in to help the team. My husband and another guest didn't feel well, so we sent everyone else off to Loch Ness while I stayed behind to care for them and clean the castle to prevent any further spread of illness. Rather than imagine the fun I was being left out of, I embraced the experience of being a real-life Cinderella without the evil stepmother. I carried buckets of cleaning supplies up and down the narrow stone steps, scrubbed floors and bathrooms, and imagined the massive leg muscles the servants must have had, even just to carry the food up and down from the kitchen.

The next day Angie had recovered, and Chad realized all he needed was to catch up on sleep, so we all pitched in to get the retreat back on track. Angie and Chad disappeared into the kitchens while Randi gathered guests for yoga to clear our minds for writing.

After getting a flashback during yoga at the Haven retreat I swore I'd never do yoga again, but Randi talked me into it. She'd seen me have a flashback in public at an event we'd both attended so I knew if anything happened, she'd be able to handle it. I decided to give it a try.

I listened to Randi's voice and relaxed with the other participants. About ten minutes later I began getting dizzy. I stopped and sat still to let the sensation pass. The air seemed thin, like there wasn't enough oxygen. I took deep breaths, reminding myself I was safe and my husband was nearby.

The next position looked easy so I shifted my palms to the floor in front of me and swung my feet back to rest my knees on the floor. In the position of a dog, horrible emotions crashed into me. I shifted back into a sitting position, clamped down my emotions and sat perfectly still. I focused only on holding myself together while the others in the room continued their yoga positions.

Randi finished and the other participants began talking. I stayed still with my eyes shut. After five days in close proximity, they knew something was wrong. My new friends gathered to offer help, but Randi took charge.

"What do you need?" she asked. Her calm comfort broke the dam holding back my tears and they began to fall.

"I'll be fine once I cry it out. I just need you to stay with me."

She shooed the others out of the room and closed the door. She sat cross legged in front of me and held my hands while I allowed the pain and emotions of one of Bishop's rapes wash over me.

"Just breathe," Randi calmly said. "Let it all out."

At home on my own I struggled to let go of my emotions, but sitting with Randi I was able to endure the pain without flinching. I don't know how long we sat there while I processed my pain. Eventually, the feelings receded and I opened my eyes.

Randi looked back, emanating love, peace, and concern. "What do you need now?"

"I just need Chad."

"I'll go get him for you." Randi wrapped her arms around me.

"Thank you."

"You're welcome." Randi stood and left the room.

Soon Chad entered and sat with me while I talked about what had happened.

Later that night as I waited for sleep, I realized that I'd been afraid of travel, flashbacks, and falling apart all these years but now that it had happened, I realized there was nothing to be afraid of. I had a flashback in front of both strangers and friends in a foreign country. Instead of embarrassment or shame, all I felt was peace and comfort.

The last stop we made before heading to London was to the Blairgowrie cemetery. The late-afternoon sun shone through the clouds as we walked up and down among the neat rows of headstones searching for ancestor names. In addition to the joy of the hunt, an absolute sense of peace settled over us. We had not arrived early enough to get a cemetery map, but there were enough Frasiers that it never took long to discover another name. During a break in the traffic passing the cemetery, the sound of bagpipes floated toward us on the wind. When it was time to leave, we'd barely covered a third of the large graveyard. I knew I needed to return someday. My soul had connected with the ancient land of Scotland.

For years I'd lived in envy of those who took vacations, but I'd always made valid excuses for why I couldn't do the same. In a departure from the norm, I'd thrown the excuses away and decided to go to Scotland. It was that simple.

The next morning, we returned our rental car and boarded a train to London. At King's Cross Station, we entered a world teeming with people.

We rode to the top of the Shard and looked out over the city of London from seventy-two stories in the air, and for the first time my fear of heights didn't manifest at all. We wandered the Tower of London and saw the magnificence of the crown jewels. We stepped foot into Westminster Abbey and allowed the hush of the ancient burial and worship grounds to surround us. And we ventured out onto the Thames in a ferryboat, concluding the day with a double-decker bus ride through the rest of the city past stunning and varied architectural delights.

And while those sites were amazing, it was the subtle things that changed my view of the world: chatting with an English couple on the train, flipping through the channels to see a newscaster with half an arm, watching a segment on tackling child abuse. I'd narrow-mindedly seen England as a far-off place where selfish people rarely attended church and didn't want children. Instead, I found a country far more accepting of others than back home, a country full of people like me who loved their families, cared about others, and looked deeper than the outer shell of a person.

Without the pain of healing, I never could have experienced the awe of Scotland and London. I would have moved from one anxiety-producing experience to another, worried about looking bad and wishing to be safe at home. Every bit of pain was worth those ten days of travel abroad.

When I got home, life crowded in again. Gavin began a new school where he would have the support he needed to continue his own journey of healing. And the days blurred from one to another in a rush of things to do, but I managed to keep the souvenirs of my time in Europe around me to remind me of the broader world and experiences that were possible.

Working closely with Angie required attending something called the Landmark Forum. I wanted to wait, but Angie urged me to attend the next session because it would help me heal. I was skeptical, having no idea what the Landmark Forum was, but trusting Angie, I signed up.

On one of the forms I had to declare what I wanted out of my participation. I thought of Scotland, how all I'd done was decide to go and it happened. I wrote down, *Be completely healed from my childhood abuse.* I paused and then added, *Have better relationships with my family.*

If it was possible, I wanted in. If not, surely I'd get something out of it. Even though the session didn't start for over a month, I was told my forum started from the moment I declared what I wanted. I had no idea what that meant, but I knew I was desperate for healing, even if it meant I had to remember more of my past.

24

MR. ROGERS

I always hated Mr. Rogers and his neighborhood. On a Friday night, I wanted to rent a chick flick, but Chad wanted to watch a documentary about Mr. Rogers. Since I usually got my way, I relented and picked up the documentary. Perhaps by watching it I could figure out why everyone else liked him so much.

I started the movie on the television in my bedroom and settled in next to Chad. I wanted to gag at the goodness they spouted as my anxiety increased. I wiggled my foot back and forth until it tired, then switched to my other one. I pulled out my phone and began playing games to distract me as the anxiety gradually took over. I couldn't wait for the show to end. As the credits began to roll, the doorbell rang. The theme song from *Mr. Rogers' Neighborhood* played while Chad left to answer the door.

The song triggered a memory I was helpless to withstand despite the sound of my mother-in-law chatting with my husband through the open doorway.

#flashback

Everything faded to black and red. In the basement of Mr. Wilson's house, I endured waves of pain from the shadowy figures that moved around me. I tried to scream, but my mouth stayed silent. I tried to move away and then to kick, but my muscles refused. My head felt like it had been blown up like a balloon and floated above my body, making it hard to figure out how to escape.

I heard Mr. Rogers blaring from the television upstairs. I latched onto the sounds, clinging to them for sanity.

The darkness waned, and I reminded myself I was in my bedroom, safe at home, but my visceral reactions continued until I curled into a fetal position, my hands pressing into my head. Sensations of pain unlike anything I'd experienced in my life washed over me. The echo of my choice to use dissociation to survive reverberated through my head. Without dissociation, the madness would have taken over. It was my first memory of being physically trapped by the drugs.

My grip on reality loosened while the need to hurt myself roared to life. I tried to wait for Chad to finish his chat, but I became desperate.

"Chad!" I weakly yelled in a voice that barely sounded like my own. "I need help." Voices murmured, and the front door opened and shut. Heavy footfalls sounded as Chad made his way to my side.

Emotion poured out of me now that I was enfolded within the safety of the most trusted person in my life. I wanted the flashbacks to stop. Not only so I had room to breathe again but so I'd know there was an end to the pain and suffering I'd endured as a child.

The next day, I called for an appointment with my trauma therapist but had to wait for two weeks. While I waited, I began searching the types of drugs used in ritual abuse to see if anything matched what I had experienced. Even though I knew something had been injected into me and I had evidence of being given drugs, it didn't make sense. How could my parents not know I was being given drugs?

I scoured the internet, reading articles across a dozen websites, from WebMD to the DEA to RAINN.

I started with the date-rape drugs Rohypnol, GHB, and Ketamine. Normally they were put into drinks. I remembered him giving me sodas sometimes, but I also clearly remembered being given shots.

The effects of Rohypnol matched up, causing loss of muscle control, slurred speech, and partial to full amnesia, but Rohypnol and GHB stayed in the system too long. My parents would have noticed when they picked me up from my playdates, so I scratched them off my list.

Ketamine was mainly used on animals, but we'd lived in a rural area where that would have been available. Under its influence, a victim might be aware but unable to move, fight back, or even speak. It could cause amnesia and hallucinations. I didn't have any memories of hallucinations unless evil spirits counted.

I looked into the stimulants, but they didn't match at all. Hallucinogens would have made me happy, not feel pain, see things that weren't real, and cause some arousal, though not as much as a stimulant, so I knew it wasn't hallucinogens. I kept searching.

Hidden amid paragraphs of information, a tiny sentence popped out at me and stopped me cold. Manipulation of certain drug commonly available in the eighties and a specific administration matched my experience. It was the technique of manipulation that caused it to take effect in five minutes and lasted about an hour. My parents would have never known I'd even been drugged by the time they picked me up. (I am purposely not disclosing the specifics.)

Not only did the drug itself match what I remembered, the list of side effects was like seeing a partial list of my own chronic health issues—fatigue, memory problems, irritability, constipation, dizziness, loss of interest in sex, and muscle weakness. I wondered if my body had been reliving the experience of the trauma for years, trying to get my attention.

The puzzle pieces fit neatly together. I'd been drugged. I wanted to beat my fists into Mr. Wilson's overgrown belly and then slam them into his face for drugging me, along with everything else he had done. How could someone hurt an innocent child like that? It defied logic.

Two weeks later, I sat in Heather's office again and shared what I had learned.

"Do we need to go to the sand-tray room?" she asked.

"What's that?"

"Have we not been to the sand-tray room yet?"

"No."

"Well, let's go and I'll show it to you."

Just steps from her office door, we entered a room with a huge table filled with white sand. One wall held tubs of different colors of sand; the other walls were filled with shelves that held hundreds of plastic and plaster figurines, trees, buildings, shells, and small toys.

Behind the office door were dark figures, like snakes and skulls. "That wall looks evil," I said.

"That is for our ritual-abuse clients." Heather gave me the rundown on the room and asked if I wanted to play.

As she talked, I spied elements around the room that spoke to me. I said yes and started gathering items that piqued my interest.

I started with a simplistic Luke Skywalker. I put his arms up over his head and pushed him into the sand, his face sticking out. I knew that wasn't right. I piled sand on top of his face and body until all I saw were his feet, hands, and a little of his arms.

I grabbed the top half of Darth Maul with his arms extended much larger than the figurine I'd put in the sand. I settled him near Luke's feet. Then I turned to another shelf and picked up an Incredible Hulk bobblehead and placed him near Luke's hands.

I went over to the section of Christmas houses and picked up a gift-wrapping store and set it on top of the plastic Luke I knew represented me. The hands and feet were still poking out of the sand on either side of the building.

I turned to the wall of evil and picked out a large, curled-up pewter dragon that was as long as the Christmas shop and set it lengthwise behind the shop. I wanted to pull down a pack of wolves, but as I reached for it, I realized there were three. I knew I could never use something that was in threes, as that was a number associated with good. Next came a cobra with a large, clear jewel set in dark pewter, which I set at the base of Darth Maul, and a hydra with its multiple serpent heads gleaming with red jeweled eyes rested next to the Incredible Hulk.

I gazed down at my scene, but it wasn't complete. I looked over at the wall of evil and settled on a stack of skulls resting on top of each other like a wicked totem. I set it in front of the shop to guard the way. It stood taller than the building and all the other evil creatures.

I turned to the Disney section and picked out Daisy Duck, Minnie Mouse, and a cute little chipmunk. I set them a distance from the horrible scene, playing together. "I'm done," I said. "Do you want to know what it means?"

"Sure," Heather replied.

I pointed to the Darth Maul and Incredible Hulk. "These represent Bishop. The dragon is the devil, and the snake and hydra are his evil minions. See how one head is broken off? If you fight back and cut off a head, two more grow in its place."

I pointed to where Luke lay buried in the sand. "That's me, though it's strange that I chose a man instead of a woman."

"The hair looks a lot like yours," Heather said.

"That's true." The man did look more like me than the women with their long hair flowing down their backs. Plus, many of them were molded plastic that couldn't move, so I couldn't rotate their hands up.

"Did you notice what building this is?" I asked as I pointed to the shop.

"No."

"It's the gift-wrapping shop. That is where you hide what is inside and only show people the pretty wrapping on the outside. They can't even guess at what's really inside. I'm trapped under there. I'm buried, even my face."

"Yes, I noticed you were careful to make sure the face was covered."

"That is because I can't be seen, and I can't talk. Everything happened in the basement, and though you can see the house and it looks nice, you can't see me and the bad things that happen in the basement." I pointed to the skull totem. "This is guarding the house so no one will discover what is happening."

I turned to the trio of happy toys. "These are all the other kids having fun. I'm angry at anyone who had a good childhood."

"That's understandable."

I looked down in sadness at what I had created.

"We're all out of time for today. Do you want to clean up, or do you want me to do it after you leave?" Heather said.

"No, I want to do it myself."

"Do you mind if I take a picture?" Heather asked.

"No. I want to take one too. Can I go get my phone?"

"Sure."

I retrieved my phone from her office and snapped a few pictures, then slid my phone into my back pocket and began in reverse order, with the Disney characters. As I picked them up with both hands, I angrily twisted them and hit them against each other, lashing out in my own small way against the unfairness of my childhood.

I set them in their places, then quickly did the same for each of the other pieces, in order. When I returned the man, I sat him up rather than the way I found him—lying down with his hands in the air.

I took a flat board and smoothed out the indentations in the sand, then drew a smiley face in the spot where they had been to erase the bad feelings the figures had conjured up. I didn't want to leave anything yucky in the room.

No wonder no one knew about my abuse. I'd made sure to bury it deep inside and smile over the pain.

25

PROGRAMMING

It seemed every time life got good, something else knocked me down. The next few days were rough. I'd opened another Pandora's box within the dark room in my soul. I constantly thought about death. I struggled to sleep, trying to stay away from the nightmares that plagued me.

I became obsessed with killing myself and making sure not to fail. I wasn't depressed or hopeless, but I needed to die. At first, thinking about it was enough, but then I had to plan. In the past, it had been a cry for help and attention, but now I was serious. I wasn't going to fail and return to the hospital. I had to succeed. I had two options—my husband's handgun or the large prescription of opioids he got for severe back pain that he never took.

I researched every aspect of my plan. I reviewed my life-insurance policy to make sure Chad would receive the money. I knew an amazing man like Chad would remarry quickly despite the challenge of our special-needs children.

I wanted to shoot at my heart but figured there must be a reason people shot themselves in the head. I needed to make sure I aimed in such a way that I wouldn't survive with brain damage. As I wondered what words to google, a flicker of my recent trip to Scotland caused me to pause. I'd just begun to learn how to live. I wanted to see more of the world.

Perhaps I could visit these places as a spirit, though it wouldn't be the same as doing it while alive. With Scotland on my mind, I fought the urge to complete my plan.

It didn't last long, however, and soon I returned to contemplating the best way to end my life. I didn't want to leave a mess for my kids or any other innocents who might be traumatized by what they saw.

If I got in my van, drove somewhere secluded, then called 911, what would happen if I chickened out and didn't pull the trigger? I'd be locked up in the hospital again.

Taking pills was the better option. It would be best if I took them with alcohol, but that would upset Chad. I began researching how many pills it would take to kill myself. I needed to make sure the bottle we had would be enough. With pills, I would feel euphoric, free from pain, and then I'd be gone. I swallowed pills all the time, so that part wouldn't be scary either. It was a perfect plan.

I showered every day, missing only when I was too sick to get out of bed. I grabbed a change of clothes, headed to the bathroom, and turned the knob. Water leaked from the edges of the knob, and it was hard to turn.

I stepped under the spray and let the water wash over me as I pondered when to take the pills to make sure the kids would have adults around to shield them.

256

I turned the water off and realized I'd been so distracted I'd forgotten to rinse the conditioner out of my hair. I twisted the knob to restore the water, but the knob fell into my hand. I stared at the broken handle and then at the water flowing from the tap. There was no shut-off valve for the tub, so I would have to shut off the water to the whole house.

All the kids were home from school for a teacher workday, and we had no water. It was more than I could handle. I texted Chad about the newest problem and curled up on my bed.

Pain and despair choked my will to keep fighting. I didn't want to remember anything else. I just wanted it to be over. The pills were my only answer.

I cried out to Jesus in my despair. *I've always believed in you, but where are you now?*

I heard stories of people in despair and God sending someone to them. It had never happened to me. In that moment, I knew I wouldn't survive unless someone intervened.

If you are there, please show me. Send someone. Anyone. A call, a text, anything. If you are God, and I know you are, show me you are real and that you care. Please, send someone to help me.

My head hurt from fighting a battle I realized I was losing. Satan was attacking me with all he had while I was most weak and vulnerable. Minutes passed, and then an hour. No one reached out.

So either no one cared or God didn't actually exist and was just a figment of my imagination. No. I knew God existed. The people who might come to my aid must have been too busy to hear the whisperings of God, too busy to care about me. Tonight, I'd wait until everyone fell asleep and then swallow the pills. I'd never wake up.

Heavy footsteps came down the hall. What was Chad doing here? He unlocked the door with the little key we kept on the doorjamb and stepped in.

"I had Dad pick me up so I could fix the shower and get the water back on." Chad usually took the train and a bus to work, a ninety-minute commute each way. It was silly to make his Dad drive all the way out there and back just to get the water turned on a few hours earlier.

He set down his laptop case and disappeared into the bathroom while I continued my silent battle. Chad came and went, telling me it wasn't the handle but the valve that was broken and he couldn't fix it and letting me know he'd called multiple plumbers but no one could come for at least two days.

He returned again, telling me he had found a plumber that could come that night. He sat on the edge of the bed, watching me, and finally said, "What's wrong?"

I sat there, my head in my hands, pressing against the pain I couldn't relieve, but I couldn't utter a word.

Chad didn't leave. I knew from experience that he would stay as long as it took.

"I don't want to tell you."

Chad remained, and the fight in my head intensified. I didn't want to die, but I needed to die. I wanted to tell him, but the words refused to come. If I said something, he would help me, and my chance would be gone. Desperate, I forced the words out against the internal fight to keep them in. "I want to hurt myself."

The dam burst, the words and the pain rushing out together. "I have it all planned out; I even checked the life-insurance policy to make sure you'd get the money if I killed myself."

The pressure eased, but the pain intensified. "It hurts so bad. I just want the pain to stop."

Chad held me while the emotions coursed through my body. "I'll take the gun to Dad's house."

"I didn't want to leave a mess, so I was going to take the opioids."

"Where did you get opioids?"

"They're yours, from when you had the back pain. There is a full bottle in the cabinet. I even checked to make sure we still had it. It's enough."

"I'll get rid of them right now."

"Okay." My chance was gone. I was relieved and upset at the same time.

Chad dropped the meds off, used the secondary locking mechanism on the safe, and then took care of the kids while I watched television. He created a buffer between my craziness and the kids, which helped me calm down and relax.

At dinnertime, he brought me some orange chicken he'd heated from the freezer. I began feeling a little more normal since I tended not to eat when I got too stressed. He brought me a dose of my antidepressant. I'd been reducing it, and probably too quickly, causing my latest issues. It was the only explanation.

I made it through the rest of the day but didn't sleep well. The next morning, I got the kids off to school.

Nothing made sense. Why had I been obsessed with death the last couple of weeks, even though I didn't feel depressed or hopeless?

I sat down with colored pencils and blank paper to see what my inner child had to say. I pulled out a blue pencil and began to draw. I drew an oval for my head and a circle for my mouth, then a stick body with a stick hand raised. I began to write.

"I, Dawn, do solemnly swear to kill myself in accordance to the laws of God if I ever reveal the sacred ordinances and covenants performed by me or any others present in this room or any other holy rooms where I participate or watch, so help me God, or God will punish me with hellfire and damnation after he smites me down like the wicked throughout history as recorded in the Bible."

I drew my other arm resting on a square and wrote, "Bible."

Often, Bishop taught from the scriptures before performing certain tests or acts, and this was no exception. He'd used the story of Ananias and Sapphira, who were each killed by God for lying as recorded in Acts 5:1–11. Other scriptures came to mind, like Acts 12:23 and Psalms 78:31, which both spoke of slaying the unrighteous. Then 2 Samuel 6:6–8, when Uzzah dared to reach out and steady the ark of God, so God killed him. Finally, I wrote down 1 Chronicles 14:16, where David had killed because God told him to.

I dropped the pencil and mulled over what I had written. The evil was incomprehensible. To use the scriptures to teach a ten-year-old child that God punishes with death and then to require such an oath was stunning, yet it brought clarity to what had been going on inside my head.

I had read that in ritual abuse, they would make one split personality promise to kill the host self if they ever spoke of what they had participated in. In the Bible, oaths were serious. Just knowing about the oath didn't mean I knew how to break it. My ten-year-old self had taken this seriously, and it had almost resulted in my death the day before. I needed to break the hold it had on my life to make sure I stayed safe.

I began drafting a way to break the oath, but it didn't seem right. With the guidance of God, I prayed and continued writing. I searched the scriptures for the things that supported what I had written.

More scriptures than I could write popped up in my search. I wrote down ten references under the words I had already written and then the words of one scripture: "The Lord worketh not in secret combinations, neither doth he will that man should shed blood, but in all things hath forbidden it, from the beginning of man" (Ether 8:19–26). I had the scriptures to back me up and knew that what Bishop had asked was not the will of God.

I drafted words to break the oath, but they didn't seem right. I alternately prayed for the right words and continued drafting until I knew I had what I needed to say.

I raised my hand, just as I had all those years ago, and placed the other on the Bible. "Through the will and power of God, I hereby break the oath the man known as Bishop forced upon me, knowing that life is sacred in the eyes of God. I also break any other oaths or promises I made to Bishop, no matter their origin or intent, knowing he was wicked and perverted the gospel of Christ, who is my Savior."

I dropped my hand. The darkness melted away, and the peace of God took its place. God had healed me again. He truly was there with me every step of the way, teaching me what I needed to do.

I was grateful for the help of my God but scared at the power Mr. Wilson still wielded all these years later. If I had followed through with my plan, it would not have been suicide, it would have been murder—with Bishop using me as a weapon against myself.

26

THE TREE

Heather wasn't surprised by the death oath, only pleased I'd figured out how to break it on my own.

"There is still something left inside, though, something that needs to be taken care of," I stated.

"How about we burn it?"

"Okay."

We had done visualization exercises before, so I quickly got into the place in my mind where we worked.

"Okay, I'm here," I said. "There is a large tree, taller than me and very wide. It is dead. There used to be leaves on it, but when I broke the oath, whatever was living in it sucked all the life out as it left. The leaves are gone, and it is just an old, dry, dead tree with black-and-gray bark. It has been chopped down. The trunk is hollow, and the hollowness extends through the branches and down the roots. Whatever evil thing I got rid of lived inside the tree, in this hollow place."

"What about your inner child? Do we need to check on her?"

My mind sought out a different place. "There were thick iron bands around my inner child's wrists and ankles, with heavy iron links strung between them."

"Like being shackled?"

"Yes. But when I broke the oath, it was like I had taken huge metal cutters and snapped a link. As soon as it was broken, the metal turned into water and dripped off my inner child."

"Where is your inner child now? Does she need a place to rest?"

I searched the playground I had created internally for my inner children, but she wasn't with the others. I found her tiny form almost hidden in a fluffy bed, high in a tower attached to a castle. "She's lying in a huge bed with thick, soft bedding piled on top of her," I said. "There are lots of people around her helping her—grown-ups who love her. One woman is almost done filling a huge tub with hot water and aromatherapy that smells wonderful."

I turned to my inner child and took a good look at her. "She is filthy. Her hair is greasy and matted, and she looks like she's been in the sewer. She is emaciated, like she's been starved. A man has already given her some gentle food her stomach can handle, and she is feeling better, but she's exhausted."

"And there are people there taking care of her?" Heather asked.

"Yes."

"Then we'll let them take care of her."

In an instant, I shifted back to the fallen tree and its stump. I knew no regular burning would take care of this tree. I picked up a gas can.

264

"I have in my hand a holy gas can. It is gasoline that is pure and powerful. I'm pouring the gasoline into the hollow stump of the tree, and it's running down, all the way to the roots. This gas can never runs out of gas; it will keep pouring until the roots are full of fuel."

For a long time, the gasoline poured into the darkness, until I wondered if it was a bottomless pit. Finally, I saw the liquid filling up the main root chamber until it came within a half inch of the top of the stump. I stopped so the gas wouldn't spill out.

"Okay. It's full. I don't want to pour gas all over the tree or it will light the other things in my garden on fire." I moved to the branches. "I'm breaking the branches off. They are so dry and brittle they break easily under my strength. I'm setting them around the trunk like a teepee."

I turned and realized that this wasn't going to work. There was too much of the tree left. With one movement, I swiped the branches away from the trunk and reached into my pocket. "I have some superglue. I'm gluing the tree back onto its trunk." I loved that I could use anything my imagination needed to take care of what I had to do. Anything was possible with visualization.

I smeared the glue on the stump and trunk, picked up the tree, and set it on its base. Then I pulled out a drill and drilled a hole halfway up the tree, just below where thick branches began veering off the main trunk. "I've drilled a hole, and now I've got the holy gas can and I'm filling up the main trunk." It took only a split second, unlike the roots.

"In my hand I have a long match, like a spear they use in jousting." I took a regular-sized match and struck it against the side of its box to light a tiny fire, then held the tiny flame up to the colored bulb at the end of my wooden spear. It became a torch.

"I held the spear up to the hole in the tree. As soon as I touched it, the whole thing went up in flames, but the flames were alive, like each tongue of flame was a worm, eating every bit of the tree to make sure it was completely consumed. It happened in a flash, but I saw everything happen as if in slow-motion. There is nothing left. Not even a speck to be blown away by the wind. It's gone."

I walked over and looked into the black void the stump and roots had left in my garden. I saw where the dirt had packed in tightly around roots that no longer existed. The hole was huge, deep, and dangerous. I thought about kicking the edges to try and fill the hole, but I worried the area would collapse and leave an ugly crater in my beautiful garden.

I noticed something in my hand—a pitcher that poured like a firehose. "I'm pouring liquid gold into the spaces where the roots used to be to fill up the hole." Gold wasn't my favorite thing, and for a second, I drew back, but I knew it was what the hole needed, so I let it pour out freely until every dark cavity was filled.

The gold went right to the top of the ground and instantly cooled and hardened. I reached down and tugged at it, causing a portion of the gold to break free.

"I pulled up some of the gold and set it in front of me," I told Heather. "It's twice as tall as I am. It looks like the sculpture from the movie *Sweet Home Alabama* when the lightning hit the sand, only it's huge, and a luminescent, shimmery gold, like a mixture of gold and glass. It's beautiful."

I stared at the sculpture that had been created as a result of doing the hard work of ridding myself of the evil tree. It was something of beauty that represented my strength.

"Do we need to go back and help your inner child now?" Heather asked.

"No," I said. "She is clean and relaxed in the bathtub and doesn't want to come out." I continued to stare at my golden trophy, even though I knew our time was over. I needed to return to my awake self so I didn't make Heather late for her next appointment. I turned to look back at the hole I'd filled with gold, but lush green grass covered the area in one seamless swath. My garden had been healed.

As I returned to awareness of my physical body, weariness consumed me. My shoulders slumped, and I inhaled a shaky breath.

I blinked open my eyes and felt the weakness in my legs, the same type I'd experienced in between my paralytic attacks. "I'm exhausted," I said.

"I can tell. That means you did hard work."

"Yeah."

"Did we talk about how the tree is a symbol of families? The roots go back while the branches go forward?"

"I don't remember, but I know that about trees."

"What you worked on helped not only you but others. Who knows how many you healed by what you did? Did you also know that liquid gold is the most powerful healing light we can use in imagery?"

"No. I don't even like gold, so it was weird that I used it, but it felt like the right thing."

"You were connecting to a higher power to heal the things you needed to heal. You did a great job; it's no wonder you're exhausted."

"It feels good, though." I glanced at the clock. "I have to go. I've already put you over time."

"That's okay. I didn't want to stop what you were doing."

I staggered to my feet, feeling light-headed.

"Are you going to be okay driving home?" Heather asked.

"Yes, I'll be fine."

I hobbled out of the office and into my van. For a few minutes, I sat, wondering if it would be better to rest in the car or get home to my bed. I chose the latter and started the engine.

It was hard to muster the energy I needed to drive, but I managed the half-hour trip. I went straight to bed, too tired to read, watch TV, or play games on my phone.

The kids woke me up when they got home from school, but I remained in bed. When Chad got home, I explained what I had done and that all I wanted was to take a hot bath and to sleep some more.

"Want me to fill the tub for you?" Chad asked.

"No, I'll do it after I rest a bit."

"Didn't you run out of bath salts?"

"I don't know, but I'm fine without them."

Chad checked anyway. "They're all gone. I'm going to go to Walmart and pick some up for you. Anything else you want?"

"Lots of red licorice."

When Chad returned, I poured the eucalyptus and spearmint bath salts into the large jetted tub. I hadn't expected bubbles, but they began growing in large white mounds all over the tub. I sunk into the fragrant water and let my body relax. I was living the same experience as my inner child, and it was wonderful.

It wasn't until the nightmares claimed my sleep again that I realized I had done more than I could have imagined possible.

27

ANCESTORS

~~~~~~

Pressure and anxiety suffocated my days, while nightmares plagued my nights. Whenever I dreamed of houses, it usually represented my internal struggles, but last night I'd dreamed of staying at a house that had been passed down through the generations. No matter how I tried to get away from the house, the needs of its past residents kept pulling me back. My husband and children were waiting in the van, wanting to leave, but I kept returning to take care of little things. Then I returned to find a murder victim.

I didn't want to be in the room with a dead body, so I went to the rear of the house, where my mother had renovated a section to create a modern, beautiful apartment. Mom was gone but had left instructions for me to get her laundry done.

The local witch screeched from beyond the front door. Mom supported the witch by giving her a few items to clean. I searched for an item that didn't need to be dry-cleaned or handled with care.

Mom was particular about how her laundry should be washed, dried, and hung.

As I frantically searched for an article of clothing with which to placate the witch, she moved to the back of the house and screamed threats. Grasping an old tee, I turned to the door just as the witch finished casting an evil spell on the house.

Investigators called out from the front of the house, wanting answers about the dead body, but I had no answers. No matter how I tried, I satisfied no one. I was overwhelmed by everything the previous occupants of this house wanted me to do before I could leave and be with Chad and the kids, who were getting upset as they waited in the car.

In this overwhelmed state, I woke up to a lazy Saturday morning. I lay in my comfortable bed for a few minutes and thought about my dream. I'd felt pressure from something outside me ever since trauma therapy. The dream had given me the answer. It came from hundreds, or maybe even thousands, of my ancestors. The message was simple, "Give us more."

It had come from pouring the liquid gold into the roots of the tree I'd envisioned. Somehow I'd stood in as proxy and in healing my own generational trauma, had healed something within them, and they wanted more The change had come from me, and so they had reached out to me, surrounding me with their urgent pleas.

I wanted to scream at them that they wanted Jesus, not me, but I didn't know how to communicate that. I mentally explored my connection to these people. They weren't in the light with Jesus, but they weren't in the darkness either. This was a void where messengers were unable to urge them into the light or the dark due to their disbelief. They remained stuck.

The spiritual beings I had previously encountered in my life had had different roles but a clear distinction of light or darkness. These beings merely displayed selfishness as mortals do, seeking what they wanted with no thought for the impact on me.

I saw my three guardian angels standing around me, their hands linked to provide a circle of protection not only from the pressures of the many but also from Satan, who pressed against the shield they provided. He stood directly in front of me and looked like an average man, slightly shorter than I was, the black holes that were his eyes sucking away all light.

It wasn't my first brush with the devil, but I'd never seen him so angry. He had always hated me and tried to claim me, but I'd always managed to slip through his fingers. He seethed about what I had done for my ancestors, giving me the clue to understanding. I had touched them when no one else could, showing them a glimpse of God's path to healing and light.

His face was full of fury, not only in the twisting of his features but in the depths of his black eyes, which held an endless supply of hatred, fear, and loathing I couldn't comprehend. I knew I was only seeing a speck of what was there, and I wanted no part of it.

I turned my head and realized that the devil had brought legions of evil beings with him. They pressed against my circle of protection from every angle. Most had never had physical bodies and were only a third to half my height. They had dark pits for eyes that were a dull obsidian rather than the endless darkness within the normal-sized heads. Their bodies were shrunken and withered by hate. They looked like dark raisins.

Even legions were not stronger than my three angels, but I wanted them gone.

I got up and focused on the mundane, physical things around me to stop thinking about the evil I had seen. I knew the angels would protect me, but I didn't like that much darkness focused on me or the voices of thousands of beings reaching out to me for help I couldn't provide.

I showered to try to wash away the experiences gripping my thoughts, but it was no use. I pulled Chad into the bedroom in the hopes he could help me figure out what to do.

At the end of my narrative, he suggested I pray and ask Jesus to send messengers to them. After all, he was the only one who had the power to help them, and it was his power that helped them before.

I knelt down at the side of my bed and began pleading for Jesus to help those in the void. After about five minutes, I realized I didn't know what to ask for or how to communicate to the people that they needed Jesus, not me. I cried out in greater earnestness that I would be given the words I needed.

I don't remember what he told me to say, but I remember what I saw. There were thousands of tiny strands of unbreakable thread connecting me to my ancestors. A pulse of energy surged out of me, causing a tiny pinpoint of light to travel along every strand out to every person who had used their agency to choose healing and was reaching out for more. That bit of communication let them know Jesus was their healer and that he was sending messengers to teach them how to move from the void and into the light, where they could heal. God had never forgotten them. Angels tried constantly to speak to them, but their disbelief had prevented them from seeing or hearing the angels. I closed my prayer with gratitude and the knowledge that Jesus would help them through their new fragile belief in him.

I began a separate prayer and, in the name of Jesus Christ, commanded all the evil spirits to leave. The legions of evil hated what I had done, but they had no choice. Jesus was more powerful than all the evil in the universe combined.

The pressure was now absent, the lingering evil gone, and I was free. I began to stand but found my legs as weak as they had been after my trauma therapy session where I'd healed the tree. I climbed into my bed to rest. The tree represented more than just my sexual abuse; it represented all the trauma experienced and handed down through the generations. I was physically, emotionally, and spiritually exhausted. In the past week, I had broken my oath to kill myself, removed the evil tree that had spawned that particularly wicked plot, and communicated with thousands of my ancestors.

My body did its own purging through nausea, vomiting, and diarrhea, sapping the last of my reserves. I stayed in bed for three days, unsure if the sickness was due to the emotional stress or if a virus had attacked my weakened body.

28

FREEDOM

A healthy dose of skepticism accompanied me to the Landmark Forum on the specified day. Explanations of what to expect at the forum were sparse and confusing. I spotted my friend Randi and sat next to her. She was my safe person, having already helped me through two public flashbacks that resulted in me crying on the floor.

I didn't know if the recent flashbacks were due to my declaring my intent to heal or part of the normal process of healing. I worried the forum might trigger another public flashback, but I focused on relaxing. *I can leave at any time. Randi will take care of me.*

Our forum leader was fun and engaging. The first thing that hit me was his explanation of the vicious cycle we get caught up in between what actually happened and the story we tell ourselves about what happened.

As I sat there, I thought about the stories I'd spent a lifetime telling myself. I had decided that the abuse was my fault because

I was never good enough to escape punishment. Even though my conscious mind had forgotten the abuse for years, the story remained. Bad things happened because I wasn't good enough and it was all my fault.

What happened was that selfish men abused me and lied to me. Hearing it ring in my head, I knew even that truth was tainted with stories I was telling myself. What happened was that I was physically and sexually abused. That was what happened. It wasn't happening anymore and hadn't happened for twenty-two years. My abusers only had the power I gave them by perpetuating their lies with my stories. I noticed I'd stopped breathing, so I forced myself to suck in air. *I refuse to allow my abusers to define who I am. I refuse to give them control over my life.*

I pondered what I'd gained by holding on to that story. Instead of hiding from the discomfort, I acknowledged it. Discomfort meant I'd gained something. No answers emerged, so I continued listening.

Human beings are racketeers—we put on a pretty face for the world while we run devastating deals in the back room. We gain things like being right, looking good, or justifying our actions in order to avoid responsibility. I rejected the idea that I ran rackets. I prided myself in taking full responsibility, which I manifested by accepting blame.

"How do we stop running rackets when we gain something by it?" The forum leader asked. "We have to understand the cost."

A slide popped up, listing the costs, such as love, well-being, and self-expression. I'd spent twenty years chronically ill. My paralysis had almost killed me. I'd kept my defenses up until I felt love only from my husband and occasionally my children. I'd learned to survive in the world by being quiet. If the costs were manifesting in my life, I must run rackets. I'd stayed quiet to avoid judgment, looking bad, and being wrong. I'd also stayed quiet to avoid getting hurt, which was a common thread in my life.

I continued to stare at the slide and read the top again. *A racket is anything that is unwanted yet persists.* Pain was a constant in my life, and I didn't want it.

How could pain be a racket? I forced myself to consider the idea. If pain was a racket, there had to be a payoff that helped me avoid responsibility. Closing off from others was justified because of the amount of pain they inflicted. The anxiety and health problems I experienced as a result of my pain gave me a free pass out of anything I didn't want to do. I avoided telling others I didn't want to participate, thus not hurting their feelings, and I got what I wanted without looking bad. It hit me like a punch to the gut. If I had used the pain in my life to avoid responsibility, I'd created the pain.

I expected everyone in my life to cause me pain. The words people chose, the way they looked at me, all got interpreted through the lens of expecting them to cause me pain. I created pain even when others didn't mean to cause pain, believing I could see past their actions to what they were actually thinking. And the vicious cycle continued, confirming to me that all people would cause me pain. What if it wasn't true but merely my way of perpetuating the lies my abusers had told me?

The only way to stop the racket was to count the cost. I'd spent my life alone, even when surrounded by people. I'd rejected friends and family. Chronic health problems plagued me for twenty years, even before the paralysis and wheelchair.

Physical pain spread from my chest to my stomach and head. I passively listened to the speaker while I accepted those sensations without resistance. The pain didn't disappear, but it lessened.

Our forum leader told us we could banish unwanted things from our lives by being present and aware. He used a participant with a headache as an example. The participant sat in a chair at the front of the room. The forum leader merely had him notice where the headache resided within his body and experience it. A headache was not good or bad, it simply was. Within a minute, the man's headache was gone. I didn't believe it was that simple, but I still wanted to try it in order to prove or disprove it for myself.

He turned to us and told us to close our eyes and choose something we didn't want. I didn't want to have PTSD anymore. I had gained a measure of control over it, but I wanted it gone.

I focused on the PTSD. It wasn't good or bad; it just was. I had to accept that it was there and locate where it was. It rested in a band across my hips, spreading down across the areas where I had been abused the most.

I sat there with the acceptance of what PTSD was, why I had it, and how it had helped me uncover the memories I needed to heal from. The moment I fully accepted this, the energy or manifestation of the PTSD slid down my legs and out my feet.

My belly felt light and airy. I opened my eyes with the rest of the group. I doubted it could be that simple, and I wondered how to know if it was truly gone, and then I reminded myself that belief was more powerful than fact. If I believed the PTSD was gone, it was gone. I let go of my natural skepticism and engaged more fully, no longer afraid of what might be coming. Even if all I got was an end to my PTSD, it was enough. The complete control the leader gave me in my own journey gave me more confidence. When the day ended, I drove home exhausted from the mental work.

That night, I followed through on a commitment I'd made to my daughter. She had spent fifty hours sewing an incredible dress patterned after the most recent Cinderella movie. I'd promised to sew on some metal butterflies and tack down the poof that went around the shoulders to give it life.

I didn't lament the late night, mourn my loss of sleep, or blame her for not getting it done sooner. I knew I had not done my part in helping her with the things she needed at the beginning and that she had worked diligently to get the dress done for the dance the following day.

It took three hours to finish the sewing and complete my promise, but, rather than irritation, I was filled with a sense of gratitude and peace. I went to bed and asked my body to give me a restful sleep for the next day.

I woke rested and arrived at the venue early, eager for another day of transformation. The forum leader talked about the defining moments, often small incidents, when we decide who we are going to be and how we can turn those things into winning formulas we use to succeed in life.

I identified the exact moment I knew something was wrong with the world. I was three or four years old and was playing in the front yard of my house near my mother, who was chatting with another woman. I looked up to see a huge black dog running at me, teeth bared, ready to rip me to shreds. I knew I was about to die.

The dog knocked me down and then ran off. I lay there, stunned but alive. I expected the adults to rush over and fuss over me and my near miss with death. Instead, I heard laughter and looked over to see that my mother was fully aware I'd been knocked down but hadn't even stopped talking.

As the years went on, I took that experience and used it to make sense of the world. I expected that at any moment, dangerous things might come charging out of nature and into my safe places to destroy my world. I also knew that the way I was expected to handle it was to pretend I was fine in the face of those horrors. My winning formula was to pretend. Pretend to be brave. Pretend to be strong. Pretend to be smart. I used it to create opportunities, and I used it to get through trauma. Over time, I pretended so much I became those things. I only needed to let go of pretending.

I was two years old when the Teton Dam broke and destroyed everything we owned, leaving me with dysentery, the clothes I wore and a few mud-stained photos. Thinking about the flood conjured the smell that permeated the area for weeks, a mix of mildew, burning cows, and churned mud. The smell brought with it a deep sense of loss and bewilderment. Throughout my life, when things were calm, I'd stood guard, bracing myself for the next catastrophe. I took on hard things, figuring it was better to choose my poison rather than wait for nature or God to hit me with the unexpected.

I already knew the way I remembered the dog attack wasn't accurate. If I'd been attacked by a vicious dog, my mother would have intervened. I asked Mom about it one day. She told me it was probably the black lab that lived in our neighborhood.

The black labs I knew were boisterous and energetic. One could easily knock down a small child in their enthusiasm. Mom probably saw a happy dog greet me and accidentally knock me down. She would have easily surmised that I was fine and expected me to get up and keep playing.

A black dog had knocked me down. That is what happened. All the rest were stories I had created around that incident. It was a tiny moment in my life, but I had created a whole persona around it.

There wasn't anything good or bad, right or wrong, about what I had done in that moment. I had chosen something, and it had both helped and hindered me in life. In identifying this, I suddenly realized the impact my choices had in creating my life. No one else did that. I did that. I chose. And if one of my choices had that much impact on my life, I could make different choices to impact my life not only in the moment but for the future.

I understood that everyone's experience at the forum was unique to them. It was like being in a personal space of enlightenment where the journey was internal and consisted of whatever a participant was ready and willing to accept.

At the end of the day, our forum leader told us we had an opportunity to become more powerful. We closed our eyes for a group exercise.

Our forum leader said, "I want you to let all the fear you've been pushing down come up."

I'd had lots of practice in letting my fears come up. I was happy to have a place to work through whatever waited inside. But nothing surfaced. The more I tried to let it come, the more closed off I became. I listened to the words of the leader and continued to try to work through the exercise, but my muscles clenched, and an impenetrable wall formed, preventing the fear from surfacing.

I reminded myself that each person was having a different experience and that we each were getting what we personally needed. I let go of doing it right or wrong and focused on being present. I heard others expressing their fear through whimpering and crying. My dissociation from those intense emotions made sense.

And so I sat in the dissociation and merely observed. Muscles throughout my body clenched, but particularly those around my shoulders, the tightness pushing in on me, cutting off my breath.

Suddenly a scream rang out. I flinched, and my attention moved from inward to outward and the waves of emotion slammed into me. People were hurting, like when I sat in Bishop's basement listening to him hurt the younger girl. I had taken her punishment. It was easier to be hurt than listen to her cries, but now I was helpless to do anything about it.

I wanted out and away, but we'd been instructed to remain in our chairs throughout the exercise. I rationalized that this was an emergency and I needed to leave. I tried to move, but my muscles were frozen. I was trapped by my body, not in the limp paralysis I'd experienced so often, but one in which my muscles had stiffened into a set position. I'd sat in the same position when I was abused, tied to a chair. I tried to open my mouth for help, but it was clamped shut.

I pushed my brain to think. No one was forcing me to stay here, sitting ramrod straight in my chair. *I'm not tied to this chair, and no one's holding me down. I can move if I want to.*

I attempted to move, but the paralysis remained. I shoved the sensation of helplessness away and tried to stay within my rational brain.

I can move if I want to.

I began with my shoulder, noticing how it was encased in imaginary cement. I managed to twitch it slightly down and back.

I focused on the other shoulder and was able to do the same, then I moved my attention to my right foot. *Push it forward; it's easy.*

I focused and struggled, but my foot didn't budge. Part of me cried out, *See, I'm paralyzed; I can't do it.* The other part of my brain responded, *Yes, you can. Just do it.*

I pushed against a great weight, and my foot finally inched forward. At that moment, I broke through the dissociation and whatever mental programming was causing this incident, and everything returned to my control. I relaxed in my chair, exhausted. I became aware of the exercise continuing around me.

"While you have been afraid of everyone around you, everyone else has been afraid of you," our forum leader said. "Isn't that funny?"

While giggles rang out across the room, tears coursed down my cheeks. I cried for all those who walked around afraid of me. I cried for everyone I'd walked around afraid of. I cried for the power and control that extended years beyond my abuse.

When I opened my eyes, I was a new person. No matter what, my abusers no longer had control over me. I knew I was in complete and total control of myself and the way I interacted with the world.

I turned around, beaming, to declare to Randi, "I'm healed. I did it."

Later at dinner, I told Chad what had happened. He looked at me with tears in his eyes, seeing the healing that had taken place.

My skin felt loose, and there was light and space in my body that hadn't been there before. The wonder-filled eyes through which I'd seen Scotland returned. I saw my children as little people struggling with their own stories about how dangerous the world was, and compassion filled me.

I mended the connections I had broken when things became so difficult. My brother didn't answer his phone, but I left him a message, wanting to leave all the horrible feelings behind and return to loving my brother. I reached out to many people, expressing love and gratitude, apologizing where I needed to, and healed the part of me that was alone by my own choice.

My future was wide open, and I looked at the world like a newborn in wonder and awe. When I broke through my fear at the Olympic Park, it was like seeing the world in color for the first time instead of in black and white. No longer was I seeing life on a flat screen; I was in the world, embracing it with a deep sense of gratitude. I had never allowed myself to explore the possibilities of my life, but now anything seemed possible.

After I left the mental hospital, I had written, "Surrounded by brokenness, I felt the difference. I shed my armor, declared I was a survivor, and walked naked into a new hope. Only then did I become a thriver." Becoming a thriver had been my goal all along.

Despite what my brother had said, I'd never wanted to be a victim. I'd become a survivor when I'd attended group, but I didn't like the idea of merely surviving. I'd spent my life surviving. I wanted to thrive.

In declaring those words, I had created that reality. I had lived lesser meanings of them as new waves of healing changed me. Walking out of my forum, I knew I had never truly understood the power, never truly lived the fullness, of that statement until I'd broken the chains of the abuse and was walking naked into a new hope.

Now I am a thriver.

EPILOGUE

As I replay my memories, I find that I go back to different versions of myself. When the ritual abuse started, I split into two little girls who didn't know each other, like twins separated at birth. It is part of the dissociative amnesia and a tool the brain uses to deal with trauma. I see the innocent ten-year-old girl who got to live at home with her family:

#memory

Dawn sits cross-legged on the carpet of her quiet house, looking down at a paper doll. She hears the engine of her brother's motorcycle fade into the distance. Everyone is gone except her sister studying downstairs. She plays alone. A loud noise causes her to jump to her feet before she realizes what she's doing. Laughter rings out, and she swings around to playfully hit her brother in the arm. He laughs as he explains that he killed the engine on the motorcycle and returned to scare her. The little girl wishes she could have seen the impressive jump, but as always, her brother gets all of the fun.

There is a hint of sadness in her, but I don't know if it's from peripheral knowledge of the ritualistic abuse or the struggles at home.

The brain uses dissociation to survive. While I don't fully address it in this book, I came to realize that part of the reason I function at such a high level is because my brain split the trauma into separate parts within itself. Those alters, or parts, remember things I can't remember. They did things I wasn't strong enough to do. They are all part of me, but some have their own belief systems and amplified aspects of my personality. My therapist knew I had Dissociative Identity Disorder long before I was willing to accept it.

Unlike in the movies, I am co-conscious with my parts, and we work together to keep me safe. I still work with my amazing trauma therapist, Heather, in the continuing process of healing. For every broken piece I find, I have help to glue it back into the whole of who I am, like the kintsugi bowl I created at the Haven Retreat. It's hard sometimes, but the rewards of healing are worth the difficulty.

The dissociation explains why my family didn't realize what was happening. Mom took me to a play date every week so I could play with my friend Melissa at a trusted church member's home. I begged her to take me, not because I was eager to go back, but I'd learned the consequences were horrible if I failed to show up, which only happened once. It has been hard for them to discover the truth. Mom looks back and sees the signs, wondering how she didn't see what was happening, but she never expected it to happen to her daughter. My parents wish they could turn back time and protect me. The stories make them sick.

No one can change the past. My parents' support manifested in their willingness to believe me, even if it was painful for them. Sometimes I thought I was crazy, but I'd ask Mom a particular question, and her memory would verify events. Mom recalled the conversation where I told her how Kyle's mother had yelled at me for playing games. I have never blamed her for not understanding what kind of games they were.

In being willing to search her own memory and face the fact that she didn't protect me, Mom helped me more than she can understand. I wanted to deny the horrible memories, even though they felt true to the depth of my soul. Healing doesn't happen in denial. I needed to accept what happened in order to begin the process, just as every victim needs to be believed to become a survivor.

I discovered that I didn't need to cut off contact with my family members. When one butterfly moves and upsets the balance of the mobile, if that butterfly stays strong in her new place, the other butterflies will adjust to the new position. I can't control if they accept the new me or not, but life has been better as I've given them the chance to get to know me.

My body and mind held the cancerous secrets of my past, spreading destruction beneath the surface until my body stopped working and I ended up in a wheelchair believing everyone would be better off without me. I fought my way from sickness to health because the cost had become too great. In making that choice, I was ready to hear what my body had been trying to tell me for years.

My therapist talked about peeling back memories like the layers of an onion. What I didn't realize was that the healing came layer upon layer as well, gradually building me up to who I am today.

I made the decision that I didn't want to crawl through life taking what I could from the world like a fat caterpillar who is never satiated. I hid in my dark cocoon, believing that I'd emerge different. I didn't know what the result of my transformation would be. I could have come out a moth, been plain, or stood out enough someone would capture me and pin me up for display.

I withdrew and did what I needed to do because that was my path. When I sat in my own caterpillar soup, I didn't feel the coming transformation, I felt destroyed. Even as my own coded discs began forming the parts that would give me wings to fly, I was only focused on trying to survive the loss of my sense of self. Only afterward could I look back and realize I had all I needed within me the whole time. Even the hungry caterpillar has a purpose, to fill itself with the strength it will take to get through transformation.

When the darkness felt binding, I struggled to break free. And I did. I emerged from the darkness and felt the fresh air around me. I stretched to let the sun warm my back and that is when I felt my wings for the first time. I paused, uncertain if I wanted to risk taking flight. The world is big and dangerous. A butterfly is fragile.

My hesitation only lasted a moment. I flew free and every bit of my journey was worth it. Part of my purpose is to share the beauty of what I discovered, the beauty that God understood and saw all along.

It is scary to show the world the unique butterfly of who I am, but I still follow the words of my coach, "Be afraid and do it anyway." Fear is a black curtain. I only discovered how flimsy it was when I brushed it aside to step into the light.

Each day power moves within me—God's power to change the world, one person at a time. Dreams have opened up all around me. I'm living a life I never imagined possible.

The memories didn't stop surfacing after I broke the hold of phantom abusers and released the manifestation of my PTSD, but I have more control over when and how they surface. I face them with the strategies I have learned, the support I have, and the ability to gain insight and healing from them. Much of what I experienced is not in this book, it is too dark and twisted. I don't want to spread that type of evil.

Don't give up. I am telling you right now that the struggle is worth the reward. You can find complete healing if that is what you truly want. If you only want to experience part of the pain and accept partial healing, that is fine too. It's all up to you and what you want. No matter what you choose, it's not wrong. This journey was right for me.

I tried to fill myself with marriage, men, and children, but nothing could fill the emptiness inside me. It was the love and light of God and his total acceptance of me that allowed me to be filled and project those qualities back out into the world. I had rejected my inner self and let it shrivel to almost nothing. I had to nourish it and help it grow until it filled the empty cavern of my flesh. Only then could I reflect God's light.

I needed to remove every last bit of the poison within me, and I needed help to do that. I needed God. I don't know where my quest for religious truth will eventually lead, but I have the rest of my life to figure things out. I have God with me, and that is enough.

I don't blame The Church of Jesus Christ of Latter-day Saints for the evil Mr. Wilson inflicted on me. Many people throughout history have taken certain teachings, split off from the main body of a specific church, and created their own religious cult. Mr. Wilson's abuse of me had nothing to do with Mormonism or Christianity. A religious cult taught him how to do what he did, perhaps for the child pornography that was created during the abuse. Unfortunately, pornography is a huge money maker. Where there is a market, supply will be created.

I struggle at times to be a part of my chosen religion, but it's gotten easier. As in many churches and places around the world, there is a culture of disbelief, victim blaming, and mishandling of victims when they come forward. It will take time for that culture to change.

I'm rarely anxious sitting inside a church anymore, despite how intertwined religion was with my abuse. I've managed to separate many of the cult's lies that have been joined to truth with the help of Christ and his atonement.

I did not lose my faith in God, though I was often angry at Him. I cling to my faith when I'm unsure of anything else. I often remind myself of the story of the wheat and tares from Matthew 13. The wheat was planted in the field, but in the night, an enemy of the farmer planted tares, or harmful weeds, in the field. The wheat and the tares looked similar, so there was no way to pull only the weeds out. The farmer had to let the weeds grow with the wheat until the harvest, when the threshing process would release the kernel of wheat and the rest could be destroyed.

Mr. Wilson planted harmful weeds in the garden of my mind. My field has grown, and now I am gathering everything and allowing only the kernels of truth that will nourish me to fall down and be gathered up. The process is giving me greater truth in my life, as well as compassion for all those who are struggling and searching for peace.

I've learned to have compassion for myself. I take more time to recover after a flashback, more time to enjoy life, and more time to spend with my kids. I have what I've always wanted—joy and peace, even if those feelings are fleeting at times.

Find a trauma therapist or trauma center. Find a support group near you. Be open to the amazing techniques available to survivors. Reach out to those around you. Reach out to me on my website at www.dawnbradford.com or through social media. It doesn't matter how great or small you feel your trauma is, it is all trauma, and you do not need to suffer alone.

I promised to be the voice of the victims of my abusers, but I also feel the need to be a voice for all victims. It is for them, and for you, that I've written my story. No matter what happened to you, no matter how bad it was, no matter how damaged you feel, complete healing is possible.

I am whole. I am healed. I am beautiful.

I am not broken.

Neither are you.

ACKNOWLEDGMENTS

This book would not be in your hands without the support and encouragement of my tribe. Chad, you anchor me and believe in me no matter what storm is blowing. I still owe you a vacation. Mom, you are more amazing than you know. "Heather," I'm blessed to have been a part of the groundbreaking trauma therapy you and others are creating. "Susan," years of foundational work with you prepared me for this journey.

All my friends at Calliope Writing Coach, you kept the crazy at bay and read all my confusing early drafts to get me to this point. Angie, you were as integral to my healing journey as you were to my writing journey. Thanks for being my Yoda. The team at Eschler Editing and Scrivener Books, thanks for adding the professional polish and making everything look as good as I hoped it would.

Finally, thank you to all the victims and survivors I've spoken with over the years. You have lifted my spirits and inspired me. You might have thought I was helping you, but I assure you it was the other way around.

Note to the Reader

If you would like to download my recommended reading or current resources lists, please visit www.dawnbradford.com. You can sign up for my newsletter and find links to my social media, @sdawnbradford, if you are interested. I love to hear from my readers. If you want to share your story, ask questions, or book me to speak, please email me at sdawnbradford@gmail.com or via my website.

If you have time, I'd love an honest review on Amazon, Goodreads, or Barnes & Noble. Reviews provide visibility so my book can find its way to others who need the message it contains. If you've recommended my book to someone else, thank you!

ABOUT THE
AUTHOR

S Dawn Bradford is a life coach, writing coach, and international public speaker. She writes fiction and nonfiction, using her life experiences to contribute to the public dialog about abuse. When Dawn is not writing or working, she enjoys hiking in the mountains, learning new things, and traveling. She lives near Salt Lake City with her amazing husband, a fluctuating number of children, and her red goldendoodle, Ginger.

Made in the USA
Monee, IL
10 September 2020